PHAIDON GUIDE TO
FURNITURE

PHAIDON GUIDE TO
FURNITURE

ANDREW BRUNT

A SPECTRUM BOOK

Prentice-Hall, Inc., Englewood Cliffs, New Jersey 07632

Library of Congress Cataloging in Publication Data

Brunt, Andrew
    Phaidon guide to furniture.

    "A Spectrum Book."
    Includes index.
    1. Furniture.   I. Title.
NK2230.B78   1983   749.2   83-3320
ISBN 0-13-661967-3
ISBN 0-13-661959-2 (pbk.)

Frontispiece: The *Bureau du Roi*, by Oeben and Riesener, 1760–69.

Originally published by Phaidon Press Ltd,
Littlegate House, St Ebbe's Street, Oxford

Planned and produced by Equinox (Oxford) Ltd,
Mayfield House, 256 Banbury Road, Oxford OX1 7DH, England
Copyright © Equinox (Oxford) Ltd, 1978, 1983
Printed in Hungary by Kossuth Nyomda, Budapest

This edition © 1983 by Prentice-Hall, Inc, Englewood Cliffs,
New Jersey 07632

A SPECTRUM BOOK

This book is available at special discount when ordered in bulk
quantities. Contact Prentice-Hall, Inc, General Publishing
Division, Special Sales, Englewood Clifs, N.J. 07632.

10 9 8 7 6 5 4 3 2 1

ISBN 0-13-661967-3

ISBN 0-13-661959-2 {PBK.}

Prentice-Hall International, Inc., *London*
Prentice-Hall of Australia Pty. Limited, *Sydney*
Prentice-Hall Canada Inc., *Toronto*
Prentice-Hall of India Private Limited, *New Delhi*
Prentice-Hall of Japan, Inc., *Tokyo*
Prentice-Hall of Southeast Asia Pte. Ltd., *Singapore*
Whitehall Books Limited, *Wellington, New Zealand*
Editora Prentice-Hall do Brasil Ltda., *Rio de Janeiro*

CONTENTS

CONTENTS

PREFACE

This book serves two main purposes. In explaining the technical and stylistic development of furniture, it provides a wide-ranging introduction to the subject for the layman, and a useful reference source for the expert. It is organized so that the reader can easily identify the period and style of a piece of furniture. To increase his enjoyment and appreciation of the subject, there is a brief description of how different societies produced differing kinds of furniture to suit their needs.

The book is divided into two main sections. The introduction deals with materials and techniques, from the first primitive hollowing of wood to the most sophisticated machine production. There is a note on how to recognize, and avoid, fakes, reproductions and repaired pieces. The guide itself explores the historical development of style, from ancient to modern times, concentrating on those periods from which the reader is most likely to find examples, whether in shops or museums.

Each section is illustrated with a variety of photographs and drawings. Some of the drawings are of individual items of furniture; others are of a series of, for example, chairs, showing stylistic changes over a period of time; yet others show how styles subtly changed when taken to different countries. A special feature are the large "panels", which neatly pinpoint the main features of a style, making it easy to tell the date and period of a piece of furniture at a glance. Photographs range from decorative details to complete room settings, showing the stylistic, and social, context of pieces of furniture seen individually elsewhere.

INTRODUCTION

Furniture gives us a more intimate impression of man's changing way of life through the ages than any other form of artifact. Since it is always created to cater for the requirements of a particular society it can imply a great deal about the nature and priorities of that society. The simplicity of Shaker furniture and the rich monumentality of the works executed by Boulle for Louis XIV indicate two very different attitudes to living. Shaker furniture, pared of all carving or decoration, reflects the spare ascetic ideals of the sect which made it; it has been described as "a religion in wood": in contrast, Boulle's furniture suggests the worldly power that Louis XIV claimed for himself and the elaborate taste of the court that surrounded him.

But the inferences drawn from a piece of furniture depend also on the function for which it was made, and how well it seems to serve that function. It must not be forgotten that ideas of functionality change. In the 20th century the job of an armchair is considered to be the provision of a comfortable object in which to relax; in other centuries its function was to act as a badge of rank. Comfort was secondary or hardly considered at all. The Coronation Chair in Westminster Abbey does not invite anyone to curl up with a book.

The study of furniture not only supplies us with an insight into differing modes of life, but also with considerable aesthetic pleasure. This pleasure is not the same as that to be gained from the greatest works of painting or sculpture. That is not its job. It is part of the background of living, not an exploration of life itself. At its best, though, furniture offers scope to enjoy the marriage of fine design and fine craftsmanship; it is with that marriage and the changing social forces that molded it that this book is concerned.

Techniques of construction

Wood is the most commonly used of all materials for furniture making. The most primitive ways of working it are by burning or hollowing, but both methods are wasteful. In Egypt, where wood was scarce, sophisticated techniques were being used by the early dynastic period (c3100–2890 BC). However, after the fall of the Roman Empire this primitive method of making furniture returned in parts of Europe, particularly for making chests.

When the construction of furniture required pieces of wood larger than those supplied by a single section of a tree it became necessary to find a way of binding together separate pieces. The easiest method of joining two pieces of wood is to tie them at right angles to each other with some form of fibrous or leather thonging; but the resulting frame, whether for a building or for a piece of furniture, needs in-filling. For a primitive house this can be done with mud and straw, but furniture requires planks, preferably of a common size. Originally these were made by driving wedges into a tree trunk to split it along the grain. The planks were then cut roughly to size and smoothed with an adze. But this, the oldest and most versatile of wood-working tools, is far from ideal for cutting across the grain to reduce planks to a required length. It consists of a metal blade set at right angles into the end of a wooden handle, which can be of various lengths but is usually about three feet long. The tool acts as a wide chisel, removing sections of wood to produce a worked but not completely flat surface. For cutting across the grain a saw is much more efficient. The Egyptians were already using saws at the beginning of their history; seven examples have been recovered from a single First Dynasty tomb. Although its use seems to have been limited in post-Roman Western Europe, the furniture shown in manuscript illuminations suggests that it never disappeared completely.

In the last 200 years technological development has

Left: A mid-15th century painting of a joiner's workshop, showing the wide variety of tools available at the time. They include two planes, chisels, awls, mallets and an early form of brace and bit. His work is fairly ornate; the pieces of carved wood at the back of the shop have Gothic pinnacles on them which are close to the architectural styles of the time.

Below: Egyptian carpenters at work, c2500 BC, from a tomb wall.

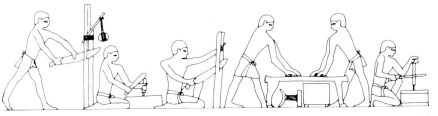

MATERIALS AND TECHNIQUES

been so rapid and so widespread that it is a shock to realize that, except for the introduction of power tools, there has been little real change in the technology of woodworking for 2500 years. The Egyptians possessed a selection, not only of adzes and saws, but of chisels, mallets, drills and smoothers too. It is not known when or where the lathe was invented but turned legs were in use before 700 BC and were introduced to Greece not long after that date.

Furniture makers are divided now into three basic groups: carpenters, joiners and cabinet-makers. This division is based historically on changes in European techniques of furniture making over the last 1000 years. Roughly speaking the work of the carpenter was superseded by that of the joiner and this in turn gave way, for some sorts of furniture, to the work of the cabinet-maker. It is not possible to make the same divisions for earlier civilizations with any historical propriety. In Egypt wood was so scarce, and in consequence so valuable, that from very early times furniture was made from what would now be termed off-cuts. The pieces were connected by pins and staples, which would now be expected of a carpenter's work, and by cut "joints", the work now associated with the joiner. Sometimes the piece would be veneered, as much to disguise the piece-meal construction as for decoration; veneering is at the center of the cabinet-maker's craft.

Since most primitive furniture was carved from single blocks of wood, in Europe the trade of the carpenter grew out of that of the carver. Besides making furniture the carpenter constructed houses. His technique was

Right: Six of the most common forms of joints. From top to bottom they are:
A tied joint
A halved or cross-lapped joint
A mortise and tenon joint
A scarf joint held together with screws and metal plates
A dove-tail joint
A tongue and groove joint.

Below: Furniture makers from a drawing in the tomb of Rekhmire. The picture shows a number of activities in a joiner's shop. Smoothers are being used (top left), a saw (top right), a bow drill (bottom right) and a saw, knife and small adze (bottom left).

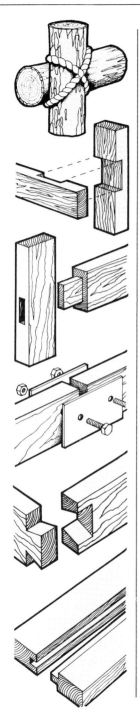

to rest beams, which could be held in place by their own weight, on walls. Where more than one floor was required, planks were nailed across the beams. A similar method was applied to making the most common form of early furniture, the chest or coffer. Planks were nailed to four corner posts, another plank or series of planks nailed on as a base and a lid attached. Extra strength was provided by surrounding the box with iron bands and security was obtained by means of bolts or locks.

Gradually, the carpenter ceased to carry out all the techniques of furniture making. A variant of his art was supplied by the turner. In turning, a piece of wood is gripped and rotated by a lathe against a blade held by the operator. Any form of round-section object can be produced by this means. Size and weight, however, are limiting factors on what can usefully be made by this method.

The turner's main occupation became chair making and it may have been from this craft that the first step was taken towards joining, since individual spokes for the legs and the back needed to be set into the seat. Holes were bored into the seat to accommodate the ends of the spokes producing, in effect, a very rudimentary mortise and tenon joint.

Joining was originally a sophistication of carpentry. It was a skill known to the Romans, which re-emerged in the 13th century in Europe. Its architectural use was in the lining of rooms with wooden paneling for decoration and for extra warmth. Nailed planks allow no leeway for swelling and contraction arising from changes in humidity or temperature. A system of grooved frames was devised made up of relatively narrow wooden members joined together with mortise and tenon joints, and with the grain of the wood running along the length of each piece. Into each frame was slid a thin panel of wood. So long as the joints fitted well the construction was strong and allowed sufficient give for the panel to shrink or swell. By using this method chests could be much lighter than the planked variety and just as secure and chairs could be paneled for extra dignity and as a protection against draughts.

Slowly the carpenter was relegated to working solely on house construction or as a specialist shipwright or wainwright. Furniture making became the business of the joiner. In 1371 the joiners of Paris seceded from the Carpenters' Guild and formed their own guild. Turners

13

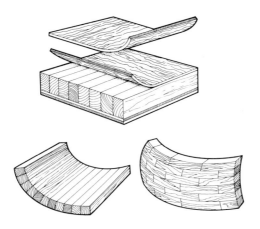

Left: Three examples of cabinet-makers' panels:
Top: the inner core of wooden rods is arranged with the grains running in parallel. The veneers are placed so that the central veneer's grain runs across that of the core and each alternate veneer runs in parallel with the core.
Below left: the core of a panel curved in one direction; the wooden blocks have sides cut at a slight angle.
Below right: the core of a panel curved in two directions. For strength the segments are assembled like a wall.

Right: A 16th-century print of eccentric turning. It shows a man working the ingenious device for producing the curious asymmetrical objects seen on the shelf. The machine is driven by a foot lathe, and the man uses an arm rest, partly because of the weight of the long chisel handle, partly to give him more control over the cutting.

remained within the Carpenters' Guild. Within the Joiners' Guild specialization became necessary as demand for a greater variety of furniture types developed. The two major divisions were chair-making and cabinet-making. Cabinet-making evolved a revolutionary technique: veneering.

Veneering had been employed in the Ancient World but thereafter fell into disuse. It consists of glueing thin layers of wood to a wooden carcase. Initially joiners' methods of construction were used for the panels which were to be veneered but these were found to be far from ideal. Only one side of a joiner's panel can be made flush. Veneering is easiest and looks best on a flush surface, but if a veneer is applied to only one side of a panel the shrinkage of the glue will make the panel warp in such a way that it will become concave on the side to which the veneer is attached. Both sides of the panel need to be veneered to avoid this. The solution was to make a panel of a series of rods of wood glued together to form a flush surface on both sides. In order to ensure that the panel remained stable two layers of veneer were applied to each side, with the grain of one veneer running across the grain of the rods and that of the second veneer running parallel to their grain. Such a panel is stable, being equally strong in each direction.

By cutting the rods at a slight angle it was possible to produce a curved panel, and by cutting the angled rods across and angling the cuts the cabinet-maker could make a panel which was curved both horizontally and vertically.

Veneers were originally cut with a saw. When true

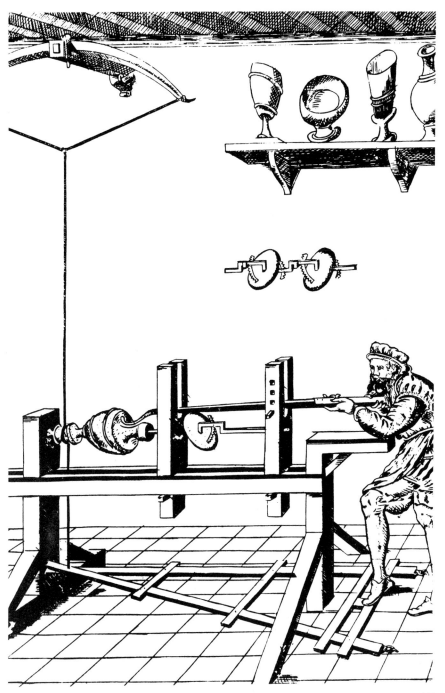

A French 18th-century illustration of a joiner's workshop. Two of the workers are using saws to cut wood which is secured to their benches by clamps. Outside, a man is stacking planks for seasoning. The sloping roof is to protect the wood. At the back of the shop a man is using a drill; near him another joiner is smoothing wood, fixed in a conventional vice.

Right: A Thonet bentwood rocking chair c1870. Michael Thonet set up a factory in Vienna in the 1840s. He perfected the steam-heating and molding of wood to produce bentwood furniture. Birch was often used. The furniture was sometimes painted a plain color, usually black, or left in its original state.

veneers were first cut in 17th-century France two or three sheets were produced for every centimeter of thickness of wood. (True veneers are defined by the thinness of the wood, in contrast to the ebony originally used in 16th- and early 17th-century Europe). By the 19th century the circular saw could cut up to six sheets from the same volume. Nowadays veneers are cut as thin as 0.6 of a millimeter. Since sawing is wasteful of wood, fine veneers are now produced by slicing sheets from a log section with an angled blade. On the other hand, 90% of veneers are made by rotary cutting: the log is rotated on a lathe against a knife which "unrolls" the log, layer by layer. This method is very useful for plywood manufacture but produces a veneer without interesting figure and so is useless for decorative surfaces.

In the 20th century veneers in the form of plywood and laminated wood have provided the basis of a vast quantity of the cheapest furniture and of some fine design. Both forms are made by glueing veneers together under pressure. In laminated wood the grains of

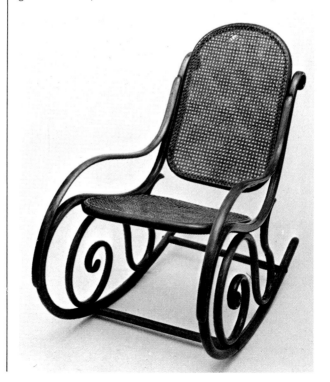

the veneers are all placed in parallel, the end product being much stronger than a solid piece of wood of the same dimensions and far more versatile. Whilst in process of being glued the laminations can be bent in steam heat and when dry will hold their shape. Since the 1920s a number of elegant but sturdy chairs and tables have been made in this way.

In plywood the grain of each sheet of veneer crosses that of its neighbor at right angles. An odd number of sheets is normally used. Starting from the center sheet the arrangement of grains in one half of the composite sheet forms a mirror image of those in the other. The final board is called by the number of layers in its construction: for example, 3 ply and 5 ply. A thick plywood is sometimes made by attaching a veneer to each side of a core formed from glued-together wooden sections—an industrial version of the cabinet-maker's panel.

Bentwood is another type of steam-heated, molded furniture. In the 1850s and 1860s Michael Thonet, a Viennese designer and manufacturer, produced a variety of bentwood birch chairs which look forward to the Art Nouveau movement and to the Modern Movement of Le Corbusier and the Bauhaus.

Techniques of decoration

In most periods, the decorativeness of wood has been considered insufficient by itself, so it has been sculpted, or patterns made out of wood or other materials have been applied to it.

Probably the most common form of sculpted decoration used in Europe has been turning. A repertory exists of often used motifs: bobbin, bobbin and reel, spiral, double spiral, baluster, column and ring. Besides the constructional use of turned members, many of these motifs were used as applied decoration on cupboards and chests. A piece of wood was turned in the normal way and then split down the middle into two pieces which were then stuck or nailed to the furniture.

Non-turned sculpture in the round was quite frequently used on grand furniture from the Renaissance to the middle of the 18th century, when its use declined. It was often both decorative and constructional. The subjects employed for furniture sculpture range from human figures, through birds, beasts and flowers to rocks and composite subjects. In some periods and places, notably in Renaissance Northern Europe, wood

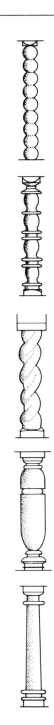

Left: Forms of turning:
Top to bottom;
bobbin, bobbin and
reel, spiral, baluster,
column and ring.

Below: Two forms of
carving. Above,
pierced carving,
below, chip carving.

sculpture was polished, the color and grain of the wood left untouched. More commonly it was gilded or painted and sometimes enameled.

The most usual ways of making sculpted decoration other than by turning have been relief and incised carving. Both forms were popular during the Renaissance, and were used on all sorts of furniture. In relief carving wood is cut away around the motif to leave it standing proud of the surface. In incised carving a design is drawn into the wood by cutting the lines which form the decoration. Two variants on incised carving enjoyed a particular vogue in Europe during the Middle Ages and the Early Renaissance: pierced and chip carving. Pierced carving was used mainly for aumbries (food cupboards). It consisted of cutting through the thickness of the wood to leave decorative holes. In the 18th century it was to be popular in England as a way of lightening the back splats of chairs.

Chip carving was a Medieval phenomenon. A geometrical pattern was drawn on the wood and small solid pieces were removed to leave a decoration of alternate sunk and raised portions.

Wood inlays and veneers have been used from the earliest recorded times. From the 19th- and 20th-century employment of the technique to mask defective workmanship the pejorative use of the word "veneer", meaning a superficial masking, has developed. The true job of veneering is to allow expensive woods to be used economically and to enable the cabinet-maker to employ woods or sections of wood which are structurally weak or very small but which are finely figured. Many of the most decorative figurings are the result of malformations in trees or come from small branches. The oyster shell veneers which were so popular in the late 17th and early 18th centuries come from olive and laburnum branches. These are too small in cross-section to be useful constructionally, and the burr woods, of which burr walnut and amboyna are two well-known examples, are produced by cutting the excrescences which develop on trees and which are structurally unusable.

The art of inlay is sometimes confused with veneering. Whereas veneer is laid on to the carcase, for inlay hollows are made in the carcase and solid blocks of wood set into them. Intarsia is a sophistication of this technique: the method is identical, but the patterns are complex and often include naturalistic pictures.

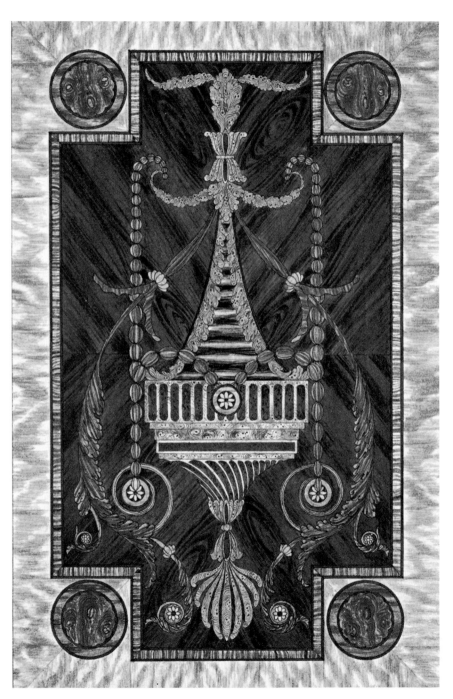

DECORATING WOOD

True veneers can be divided into four groups; surround veneers; overall veneers; parquetry and marquetry. The first modern true veneer was produced as a surround veneer. In the 16th century ebony had been imported into Europe and some furniture had been made of it. It was immensely heavy and the wood was brittle and difficult to work. In the 17th century it was cut into slices and applied, sometimes sculpted in relief or incised, to a carcase made of a lighter wood, generally oak or pine. As saws were improved, it became possible to make very thin slices, or true veneers, of ebony. The shiny black was an ideal foil for the panels of *pietre dure* (semi-precious stones) which became fashionable among the rich as a furniture decoration. In the middle and late 17th century cabinets veneered in ebony and semi-precious stones appeared in most of the great houses of Europe. Ebony was so popular that from it the French cabinet-maker gained his name: the *ébéniste*.

A surround veneer is a frame used to set off another material. Since the early 18th century one of the most commonly used methods of framing the dominant wood of table tops and commode drawers and the glazed panels or glass doors of bookcases has been cross-banding. Any close-grained wood can be employed. It is cut across the grain to the width required to form a border and each section is set with its grain at right angles to the edge of the piece of furniture.

Overall veneers have been used for most forms of furniture apart from seat furniture. The veneer is applied to a carcase of a different wood, or a particularly beautifully figured walnut or mahogany veneer is applied to a carcase of a less attractively patterned sample of the same wood.

Parquetry and marquetry are both ways of making patterns out of veneers. Parquetry is the creation of geometrical designs made of pieces of the same wood and opposed grain or of a variety of woods. A wooden chess-board is an example of parquetry. The wooden herringbone floor pattern often referred to as "parquet flooring" follows a parquetry pattern, but the pattern is made of blocks, not of veneers.

In contrast, marquetry usually involves naturalistic designs, although highly complicated geometrical patterns are often also labeled marquetry.

Many different woods are used in veneering. Already in Roman times there was a considerable number of

Left: A selection of veneers: the dates after them refer to the periods when they were most popular.

Key:
1 Satinwood: early 19th century
2 Tulipwood: 18th century
3 Burr walnut: England, very late 17th century
4 Rosewood: 18th and 19th centuries
5 Thuyawood: 18th and 19th centuries
6 Amboyna: 18th and 19th centuries
7 Zebrawood: 18th and 19th centuries
8 Kingwood: 18th and 19th centuries

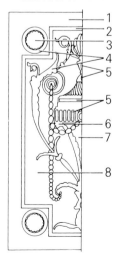

them. In 77 AD Pliny the Elder wrote that the best woods for veneers were citrus, terabinth, maple, box, palm, holly, holm-oak, elder and poplar. With the opening up of Asia, Africa, the Americas and Australasia to European trade from the later 17th century onwards a vast range of new woods have come into use. The brilliant red padouk tree, its burr, amboyna wood and the dark brown to yellow striped zebrawood are from the Andaman Islands; the deep brown and violet kingwood comes from Brazil, and tulipwood, with its great variety of shades of red, is imported from Burma. Ebony can vary greatly in color. African ebony is jet black, often streaked with brown; Ceylonese or Coromandel ebony is black with purple markings, and Macassar ebony from the Celebes varies from a dusky yellow to deep brown with a darker brown or black figuring. Walnut and mahogany show an even wider variation, depending on their place of origin.

Once a wood became available fashion dictated its popularity. Rosewood and teak were popular veneers in the 1950s and 1960s, as satinwood had been in the late 18th century. Blond woods, particularly birch, were in the ascendant in the 1840s.

The Decoration of Wood with Other Materials

Inlays and veneers of materials other than wood have been applied to wooden furniture since the early dynastic period in Egypt. The extreme ductility of gold and silver has encouraged their use as wire for inlay and as thin sheets for veneer. Silver was particularly popular in 17th-century Europe at the major courts. Sheets of it were beaten to shape over a wooden carcase, forming an overall veneer. More often it was used in the form of mounts for especially fine furniture, although bronze and brass were used more frequently.

Gilded bronze (ormolu) has been particularly popular for use on luxury furniture in Europe from the 16th to the 19th centuries. Gold leaf was sometimes applied to wooden furniture. The parts to be gilded were covered with a layer of gesso, a sort of plaster, which was then rubbed down and cut to give a crisp edge to the carved wood beneath. A second, very fine layer of gesso was added and the leaf applied just before it had completely dried out. When dry it was burnished with an agate to a high gloss. The gilding of metal mounts was usually done by placing the mount in an amalgam of mercury and gold and driving off the mercury by the

Detail of a French 18th-century ormolu mount. Cast in bronze, it was then gilded by being placed in an amalgam of mercury and gold. Heat was applied to drive off the mercury. Mounts were designed by specialists, but since mount makers did not known their destined use, the screw heads were often obtrusive. Riesener introduced mounts with invisible attachments.

Detail from the top of a Bavarian table, c1710–20. It is a piece of extremely skillful marquetry of tortoiseshell, mother-of-pearl, brass, agate, pewter and lapis lazuli. The complicated architectural vista is an unusual subject, of Baroque complexity.

application of heat; a dangerous process, the vapor from which accounted for the sickness and death of generations of gilders.

Pewter, copper, cut steel, bronze and brass have also been used for decorative purposes, with the same methods being employed, and in the 20th century, chromium and aluminum have been employed.

Precious stones have rarely been used but most civilizations have made inlays of semi-precious stones for luxury furniture. The inlay on the throne of Tutankhamun contains lapis-lazuli. Panels of *pietre dure*, mosaic pictures and patterns of semi-precious stones were a speciality of Florence and Milan in the 17th and 18th centuries. Augsburg and Prague were also centers for this sort of work.

The most regularly used animal substances for inlays and veneers are ivory, bone and tortoiseshell but leather, fish and reptile skins have also been fashionable from time to time. Business desks sported leather tops for 200 years, and in the 1920s and 1930s a range of objects from mirror frames and cupboard doors to backs of hair brushes was decorated with shagreen, which is shark skin dyed a green/blue color. Tortoise-

MATERIALS AND TECHNIQUES

Furniture has sometimes been made entirely of porcelain. In this example, the Table of the Grand Commanders, the top, column and base are of Sèvres porcelain, protected by gilt bronze. Commissioned by Napoleon, the decorations on the table represent the great military men of history. More frequently the Sèvres factory made plaques which were incorporated by furniture designers into their work.

shell varies in color from yellow through brown to red and is nearly transparent when cut thin and polished. It was popular as a veneer from the 16th to the 19th centuries and reached the height of its popularity in the 17th century. It was often backed with colored foil for greater brilliance, and occasionally dyed.

Ivory and bone have usually been left in their natural state but from time to time have been dyed. Sometimes they have been etched. On large items of furniture they have usually been employed as a thin veneer alongside woods and metals although the wood of some Indian and Ceylonese cabinets is completely hidden by carved ivory plaques. Chairs with overall ivory veneers were made for the European market in the 17th and 18th centuries. On very rare occasions ivory has been used as a structural material. The 6th-century Byzantine throne of Maxentius has survived the centuries and is made throughout of carved ivory.

Porcelain and Stoneware

Porcelain and stoneware have occasionally been used as decoration for wooden furniture and even as materials for furniture construction in their own right. In

Marble has been used as a material for table tops since the Renaissance. In this French 19th-century *guéridon* in the style of Carlin, the triangular top and lower shelf are of Carrara marble. Each shelf is surrounded by a gallery of gilt bronze.

China, where stoneware was first made c1400 BC, it was used to make pillows. In the 19th century AD porcelain—invented about 900 years earlier—was made into garden furniture: tubs for plants and barrel-shaped garden seats.

In Europe stoneware first became an element in furniture decoration in the 18th century, when Robert Adam and his followers incorporated Josiah Wedgwood's jasperware plaques in English Neoclassical furniture. French and German cabinet-makers rapidly followed suit.

Porcelain was one of the most valued imports from the East. When the secrets of true porcelain production were solved in early 18th-century Europe it became a point of prestige for any ruler to have his own factory and to be able to display its products. The King of Naples set up a porcelain factory at Capodimonte and in 1757–59 a room of porcelain complete with sconces and mirror frames was fashioned for the royal palace at Portici.

Individual pieces of porcelain furniture have been made from time to time, usually in the form of candelabra or of stands of one kind or another. An example is the biggest porcelain chandelier in the world, made at Meissen for Ludwig II of Bavaria. Porcelain is too brittle and light for most forms of furniture although three porcelain tables were made at Sèvres for Napoleon.

Stone

Stone is not a comfortable material. It is hard. Its virtues are that it lasts and it can display both rude strength and grandeur. The Egyptians used alabaster for votive tables. The Romans used marble for tables and candelabra when they wished to be particularly splendid. Renaissance princes sometimes copied the idea. The Minoans and Greeks used stone for thrones and the Greeks and Romans, very sensibly, employed it for seating out of doors, a use to which it is still put.

The tools of the sculptor have changed little over the centuries. The point or punch, the claw chisel, the flat chisel, the mallet, the auger and pumice or emery for polishing were used by the Ancient Greeks and continue to be used today. The Greeks used a method to stun the marble, producing a dull bloom and a granular surface similar to that of limestone. The Romans used a form of chiseled polishing, before the final polishing with pumice, producing the gloss now associated with

MATERIALS AND TECHNIQUES

marble. Sculpture was usually painted, but whether the same was true of furniture is not known.

From the Renaissance marble-topped tables, particularly side-tables, have graced the salons of great European houses. In the 19th and 20th centuries marble has been used as the top of tables for meat

Stone is a suitable medium for outdoor furniture. This 2nd — 4th-century BC Greek votive throne came originally from a stadium. The sculpted winged lions on the sides were a conventional decoration. Griffins were also popular.

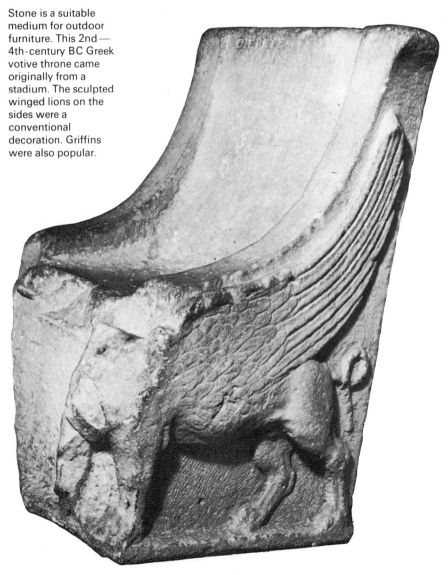

Furniture has been made purely of iron since Roman times. This 16th-century German coffer shows two of the common uses of iron in furniture. For security and strength there are the great bands and bolt holders. For decoration there is the wrought iron substructure and curved corner pieces, twisted into shapes not possible in wood since it would break.

preparation, (where the cold quality of the material is useful) and as table tops in public houses, where a durable, easily wiped-down surface is required. In the 20th century marble-topped dining tables became fashionable once again.

Artificial stone has often been popular. Scagliola, a marble paste, has provided highly decorative table tops since the mid-18th century. In the 20th century large quantities of rough outdoor furniture have been made of concrete, a mixture of cement, sand, pebbles and stone chippings.

Metals

From time to time both solid silver and solid gold furniture has been made. Most of it has subsequently been melted down. The great chandelier in William III's presence chamber at Hampton Court Palace is a splendid example of an extant piece of silver furniture and in 1662 John Evelyn described a "greate looking-Glasse and Toilet (set) of beaten and massive gold" in Queen Catherine of Braganza's bedroom in the same palace.

Bronze, produced since the early days of the Ancient

MATERIALS AND TECHNIQUES

Egyptians, has been used far more often than the precious metals but it has never been cheap either, and has usually been reserved for display pieces or for mounts. A mixture of copper and tin, bronze is a very brittle metal and is usually cast rather than hammered. For the last 300 years re-usable molds have generally been employed but the most highly regarded technique of casting is the *cire-perdue* (lost wax) method, by which the space occupied by a wax model is precisely filled with molten bronze after the wax has been melted out. This method produces a "one-off" article.

Iron is a difficult metal to extract and work with a primitive technology and it was not used to any significant extent for furniture until well into the Roman era. It was usually cast in molds but since the 18th century delightfully light-looking garden furniture has been constructed of wrought iron. Thin, heated iron bars are beaten into shape by a blacksmith with a resulting precision and delicacy of detail.

Steel has the advantage of being more elastic than iron, of retaining its strength in finer strips or bars and having a more brilliant surface. It can be cut and faceted. It was rarely used before the 20th century, although England and Russia produced very attractive steel furniture in the 18th century. In the present century designers of many nationalities have used steel bars and tubes for structural purposes.

In the 19th century brass was very popular for beds.

Six main methods have been used to decorate metal furniture: chasing, in which the surface of the metal is hammered and a punch used for detailed work; embossing or repoussé work, in which the metal is hammered and punched from the reverse to raise a pattern in relief; engraving, gilding, inlaying and enameling.

Two major methods of inlaying and of enameling have been used on metal furniture. Niello and damascening, the two forms of inlay, have been mainly used for armor, jewelry and small items like boxes and candlesticks, but they have also been used on sections of larger pieces of furniture. Niello was popular in Byzantium and in 15th-century Germany and Italy. In niello work a design is engraved. An alloy is made of copper, silver, lead and sulphur and is reduced to powder. A solution of borax is applied to the engraved object and the powder is rubbed into the design. When the metal is heated the powder fuses and fills the engraved lines. After cooling any excess alloy is scraped away. The

A modern glass table. The material is so fragile and so expensive that it was little used for furniture before the 20th century. A new way of making plate glass now enables the production of large pieces, so that the future production of cheap all-glass furniture is a possibility.

resulting design is black against the color of the surrounding metal.

Damascening, which was practiced throughout Europe in the 16th century, is the beating of gold or silver wire into a design cut into an object of baser metal, usually iron. Milan was the great center of production for panels made by this method.

Enameling is fusing glass onto a prepared surface, usually metal, and has only rarely been applied to furniture. In cloisonné enamel cells are built up of metal wire on a metal base. Glass paste is then placed in the cells and fused. In champlevé enamel the cells are cut in the thickness of the metal base. Champlevé was the more common technique in the Middle Ages, whereas at other times it has been more usual to employ cloisonné.

Glass
Except for mirrors and candelabra glass furniture is almost completely the product of the 20th century. Earlier glass technology was such that fine plate glass was prohibitively expensive for such a fragile material

to be used in furnishings.

For centuries the most common technique of working glass was blowing. Flattish glass can be produced by blowing and rotating but it is of uneven thickness and is concentrically banded. It could be used for windows but was not much use for mirrors.

In 17th-century France mirror glass was produced by laying the molten material in a table with raised sides, whose height was the required thickness of the glass. A roller was then passed over the surface of the metal. The fire-finish which gives glass its glitter and transparency was destroyed by contact with the table and the roller, a problem still found in the production of roller glass. To restore the surface the glass had to be ground and polished by hand. It was correspondingly expensive.

The fashion for glass furniture in the 1920s and 1930s was made possible by the development of machine polishing in the 19th century. The British invention of float glass in the late 1960s, eliminating the need for grinding and polishing, should make glass furniture cheaper in the future.

A 14th-century Japanese document box, decorated with a technique of lacquering known as *maki-e*. The major decoration is in gold with a sprinkling of gold dust in the lacquer itself.

LACQUER AND JAPANNING

An example of red lacquer, this is the throne of Chien Lung, made in China in the 18th century. The detailed all-over carving is in very high relief, indicating that many layers of lacquer have been applied. Each layer was painted and then allowed to dry before the next was applied, a time-consuming process. Red lacquer was a color reserved for the emperor alone when used in making beds.

Lacquer and Japanning

Lacquer was invented in China and for centuries was one of the great luxury products of the Far East.

Lacquering is the process of producing a hard, decorative surface over wood or papier-mâché by applying repeated coats of the sap of the tree *Rhus vernicifera*. The name "lacquer" derives from the Hindustani "lakh," a hard varnish produced by the insect *tachardia lacca*, which forms the basis of shellac, one of the substances used in Europe as a lacquer substitute.

The raw oriental lacquer (the sap of *rhus vernicifera*) is heated and purified. It is laid onto the base in a series of separate coats, each of which must dry before the next is added. Since in the finest lacquer there can be as many as 20 coats the process is time-consuming and expensive. The final surface is polished.

Five major ways were employed in the East for making lacquer furniture: in the first a low relief was built up from layers of lacquer and details were painted after

31

the layers had dried. In Coromandel lacquer, which, despite its name, was made in China and was in the 18th and 19th centuries the commonest form of lacquer, one or two thick overall layers of lacquer were applied instead of several separate coats, a design was cut through to the wood and colored. Alternatively, different colors were used for the several layers and pictures were carved through to leave a polychrome effect. Another technique was to cut the lacquer and inlay it with metal or mother-of-pearl. Finally, shell or mother-of-pearl could be pressed into the wet lacquer and the surface smoothed after drying. This work often goes under the name of *lac burgauté*.

Lacquer has been imitated in Europe since the 17th century. Layers of varnish were applied to wooden furniture over a gesso ground and reliefs built up of varnish and sawdust. At various times copal, gum arabic and shellac were used in place of true lacquer. The process became known as japanning in the 17th century because the lacquers of Japan were more highly prized in Europe than any others. The standard of European work did not rival that of the best oriental products until the 1920s and 1930s.

An example of European lacquering, known as japanning since Japanese lacquers were highly admired in Europe. This is an early 18th-century japanned cabinet and bureau. Although some attempt has been made to emulate oriental style in the landscapes, the floral decorations are completely Western in feeling. This combination of red and gold japanned decoration was very popular in England in the late 17th and early 18th centuries.

Basketry and Caning

For as long as human beings have used furniture it has been woven from natural fibers. Rush mats were the sole furniture of many primitive peoples and *tatami* (rice-straw) mats remain the traditional basic furnishings of the Japanese.

In basketry pliable split canes or reeds are woven around a warp of stiff rods. Basketwork or wickerwork was used throughout Bronze-Age Europe, the Ancient world and Europe in the early Middle Ages from c500–c1100 AD and returned to widespread favor in the 19th century.

Caning has usually been employed for backs and seats of chairs and sofas. Split rattan canes are interlaced to form an open mesh. During the 17th and 18th centuries in Europe, the process was refined, so that the finer the mesh the later the piece is likely to be.

Bamboo

Although bamboo is a cane and can be bent under pressure, its qualities are nearer to those of solid wood than to the cane used in canework. It was used for outdoor furniture in Southern China and was imitated in beech in late 18th- and early 19th-century England. During the oriental fad of the 1890s it gained popularity in England, France and the US.

Papier-Mâché

True *papier-mâché* is formed of paper scraps boiled and pounded into a paste with gum. It is poured or pressed into molds and when dry is suprisingly tough.

A corridor in the Brighton Pavilion, England, built for the Prince Regent between 1815 and 1821. The chair on the left is made of bamboo, the cabinets on the right are English cabinets made in solid wood and carved to simulate bamboo. The flamboyant mixture of styles reflects the exotic tastes of the Prince Regent who made little distinction between Chinese and Indian work.

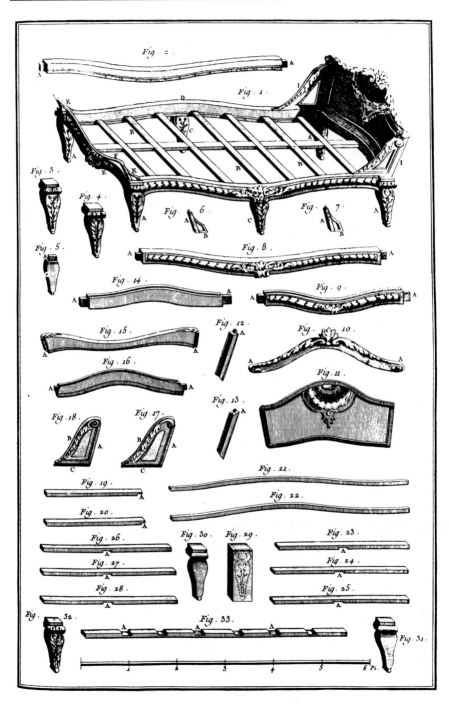

Above: A mid-19th century English sofa made of *papier-mâché*, probably by the firm of Jennens and Bettridge, who produced a vast quantity of such work. It is extremely ornate. The *papier-mâché* sheets are japanned black to imitate oriental lacquer, and it is very highly decorated with mother-of-pearl inlay.

Left: An 18th-century French print. It is a working drawing produced to show other craftsmen the detailed construction of a *veilleuse*, or daybed. Even tenons are shown, and fig. 29 shows how the outline of a carved leg was to be drawn on a block of wood.

Until the early 19th century it was used in the manufacture of sconces, mirror frames and similar decorative features. In the mid-19th century, however, both the traditionally made *papier-mâché* and laminated paper boards, which went by the same name, were used to make a wide variety of furniture which was often japanned black and decorated with mother-of-pearl.

Plastics
Although the first plastic was patented by the English inventor, Alexander Parker, in 1855, plastics have only become important in furniture making since World War II, but since that time they have had a profound effect on design.

Reproductions, Copies and Fakes
Reproductions can be defined as objects honestly described as made in the style of a specific designer or period. Copies are equally honest reproductions of an individual piece of furniture. Faking is reproduction carried out with the intention of deceiving.

In trying to decide whether a piece is genuine or not a knowledge of techniques of construction current in a given period, of woods used, of the kind of nails, screws or pegs employed are a necessary basis from which to start.

A few dates may help. Screws were not introduced

until c1675 and were handmade until 1851. The hand-made screw rarely has the slit on the head aligned absolutely centrally. It has little or no taper and a much shallower spiral than the machine-made variety. It is very rare for a screw to need replacing except on a hinge or a mount. Until 1790 nails were hand cut. They were less "correctly" made than machine-made nails. The circular saw was introduced in the early 19th century. Hand sawing leaves straight ridges whereas those left by a circular saw form an arc. Unsanded drawer bottoms were usual for all but the finest furniture until the mid-19th century and even if no ridging is visible to the eye the fingers soon learn to distinguish between the patterns left by the two saws.

However, given the craftsmanship and knowledge of the faker, a modern well-made fake will be difficult to detect on purely stylistic grounds. As for fakes made at other times, in general a piece made out of period will differ from original work in that it will show something of the taste of its own age as well as that of the age it is copying. For example, a Victorian reproduction of a carved Chippendale chair or a Second Empire reproduction of a Louis XV commode may be easily spotted, if, as is usually the case, the designer has decided to go one better than his original and include an extra bit of decoration, or, in the case of the chair, has made it just that bit slimmer and lighter than the original article. But if the "Chippendale" chair is carved by hand, the ormolu well cast from an old mold and the makers have kept to the original styles it may be difficult or even impossible to tell the 19th-century piece from its prototype. It will have gained a genuine patina from care and use and to all intents and purposes it is as good as the original article except as an object of study.

Of recent years the practice has increased of putting together "old" pieces of furniture out of odd parts from the right period, a practice extremely difficult to discern. Decorating and doctoring plain but genuine pieces to make them more attractive in the sale room has also become popular. Wood cut for a new use can usually be identified. Recut edges will have been stained to fit with the overall color of the reconstituted piece. The color will probably be too even. With use and exposure to sunlight wood mellows. Its color range changes. Parts most exposed to the sun become lighter than those which are protected. Paint fades and both paint and wood become scuffed on those parts against which people habitually brush or by which they normally lift or move a piece. Polish hardens very slowly and on carved furniture will have solidified in the deep sections of the carving. Where the polish in a deep carving is appreciably softer than that on the surrounding wood the carving is probably recent, the polish having been forced into it to make it the same color as the rest of the piece.

Top left: The *Bureau du Roi*, begun by the master cabinet-maker Oeben in 1760, and finished after his death by Riesener, in 1769. It was made for Louis XV and the style of the desk, with its cylinder top, was an invention of Oeben's. After the French Revolution Riesener was given the job of removing the royal ciphers on the desk and replacing them with decorative marquetry.

Below left: The copy—indistinguishable from the original—made by Dasson for the Marquess of Hertford in the 19th century. He also had a copy made of Boulle's desk for the Elector of Bavaria, though not by Dasson. He made many copies, a job at which he was very able. A first-class craftsman is able to duplicate even the finest work from the past.

ANCIENT FURNITURE

Sophisticated techniques, rare materials and beautiful designs characterize much Ancient furniture. The Egyptians used rich colors and expensive materials, the Greeks designed some extremely graceful pieces and the Romans—who loved grandeur—used massive furniture whenever possible.

Egypt

By the beginning of the dynastic period (c3100 BC), the bed, chair and stool, the table and the container had all been invented. Though very little furniture remains from such an early date, the Egyptian habit of supplying the dead with the paraphernalia of the living and the country's dry climate have ensured a few survivals.

More bed-frames remain than any other form of furnishing from the Early Dynastic period (c3100–2686 BC). They range from: the crudest frame with legs and side sections merely lashed together; through beds made of four bent pieces of wood tenoned into each

A crudely made early Egyptian chest. The front is made of off-cuts of wood.

Above: Two wall-paintings showing a common form of offering table of triangular section. On the left is a bull-legged stool. The chair on the right is much simpler, and was used with a cushion.

Below: A very early dynastic Egyptian table made out of a single piece of wood.

other at curious angles; to beds with well mortised and tenoned side and end pieces, carved, tenoned and lashed bull-legs for support, and slits in the side pieces for leather straps which formed the base.

Joined boxes and hollowed pieces of wood were both used as containers. Tables could be carved from a single block of wood or stone or could be constructed much like a modern coffee table, that is, with straight, separate legs, the pieces tenoned together; some have cross-overs between the legs for decorative purposes.

The bull-leg seems to have been ubiquitous and wood and ivory examples survive. Such legs were often supported on a decorative beaded cylinder a few inches high which was sometimes covered with metal. Legs for beds were only a few inches high. Seat furniture as a whole was probably lower than 20th-century furniture, partly because the Egyptians were a short people, partly because their seated posture on couches was more like squatting than sitting.

ANCIENT FURNITURE

Very little furniture remains from the Old Kingdom period (c2686–2181 BC). There are, however, a few models or pieces of furniture cast in metal for tombs and a number of excellent wall paintings showing furnishings.

Fortunately, the contents of the tomb of Queen Hetepheres, wife of Sneferu and mother of Cheops, the builder of the Great Pyramid, survive. The tomb was opened in 1925. It contained the remains of a bed, two armchairs, a carrying chair, a headrest, a combined canopy and screen and two chests. The wood of which the furniture was made had turned to dust but the furniture had been inlaid and covered with beaten gold plates whose positions when found were recorded with such accuracy that it has been possible to reconstruct some of the furniture.

The legs and rails of the bed are sheathed in gold and the foot is inlaid with faience. The legs are formed like the fore and hind limbs of a lion. From wall paintings

The bed canopy of Queen Hetepheres, from a 4th-Dynasty tomb. Curtains were hung on all four sides, of fine linen as a mosquito net, then with heavier material to exclude draughts. The bed and canopy were made of gilded wood, the lintels covered with hieroglyphics.

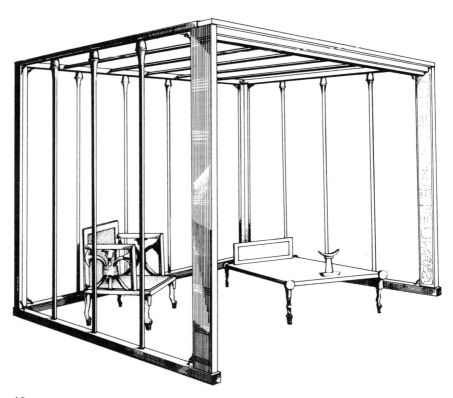

The chair of Queen Hetepheres. Made in gilded wood, the sides are formed into three lotus flowers. The shape of the legs, which finish with a paw on top of a beaded cylinder, date in style from earlier than the 4th Dynasty. The chair would have been used with a cushion.

and sculptures it is clear that this motif and a similar motif of gazelle legs were common for beds, tables and seat furniture from the Old Kingdom onwards. These motifs were later adopted throughout the Near East and much of Western Europe. The bed sloped upwards from the foot to the head, where the gold covered headrest would be placed.

The canopy screen is decorated on the outside with matt gold and on the inside with gold sheets beaten and etched with hieroglyphics giving the titles of Hetepheres' husband. One of the chests contained fragments of linen curtains fine enough to act as mosquito netting and of heavier curtains to exclude draughts and provide privacy. The complete canopy would have served the same purpose as the box-bed in Medieval Europe with the added advantage that it was mobile, being constructed for ease of setting up and dismantling. The one armchair which it has been possible to reconstruct is a piece of great elegance and sophistication. Both mortising and doweling are used in its construction and the arm-rests are beveled. Each side panel is formed of 3 gilded lotus flowers set in a rectangular frame. The legs are gold-covered lion monopodia.

There seems to have been little change in Egyptian

ANCIENT FURNITURE

furniture design during its long history except that at some unknown point during the Middle Kingdom (c2133–1633 BC) a new and more comfortable form of armchair evolved. The straight-backed version continued to be made but a false back was inserted in many examples—which retained the customary straight back—to provide a sloping support for the spine.

A fair number of pieces of furniture from the period of the New Kingdom (1567–1085 BC) survive. In particular two tombs, when taken together, provide a picture of the domestic surroundings of a pharaoh and of an officer of state of almost the same period. In c1400 BC Kha, the Overseer of Works to Amenophis III, was buried in the Theban necropolis. The Pharaoh

The Golden Throne of Tutankhamun, from the New Kingdom period. At the back are the young king and his queen, Ankhesenamun. He is sitting on an upholstered chair. The picture is made out of gold and silver with inlays of colored glass paste, calcite and ceramics. The lion legs standing on beaded cylinders are a common feature of Egyptian work. At some time panels of gilded wood have been torn out of the stretchers.

Tutankhamun's painted box, which was used as a clothes chest. The scenes are of war and of hunting. The picture on the front is of the Pharaoh triumphing over his enemies, while on the lid desert animals flee from the king. This box is one of the most heavily decorated objects found in the tomb.

Tutankhamun was placed in his tomb in the Valley of the Kings 50 years later. Both tombs were discovered virtually intact in the 20th century.

As is to be expected, the pharaoh's furniture is much richer than that of Kha but the forms of both are equally sophisticated and Kha's displays a feature which is as common now as it was to the Egyptians: the sort of decoration fashionable among the very rich is copied in cheaper materials for the not so rich. Although some of Tutankhamun's furniture was painted most of it was gilded and a good deal of the gilding was done with substantial gold plates. Much of it is inlaid with semi-precious stones or veneered with ivory and ebony. In Kha's furniture black paint replaced ebony, white represented ivory and yellow was substituted for gold. Whereas the pharaoh's pieces were often made of expensive imported woods, Kha's, with the exception of one stool, were made of locally available timber.

Throughout Middle Eastern and Western history the chair has symbolized authority. Whereas Tutankhamun's tomb contained a number of chairs, including the famous golden throne and the ceremonial chair with their exquisite inlays, Kha's contained only one: a chair without arms but with the frequently found lion legs, a plaited seat and painted decoration to simulate gilding and inlay work.

Above: A wooden folding chair from the New Kingdom. It has lost its seat, which was probably made of leather. Each leg is in the shape of a goose head, a popular motif for folding chairs. The heads are inlaid with ivory.

Below: A low stool, c1250 BC, covered with gesso, a sort of plaster, and painted white. The pattern of staves is quite common, both for stools and small tables. The seat curved in two directions is also a common form, though found less frequently than seats curved in one direction.

Stools, however, were fairly common at this time. They range from crude three-legged workmen's stools to beautifully constructed wooden lattice-work stools with concave or double curved seats. Folding stools with leather or fabric seats were in use and in the 18th dynasty, 1567–1320 BC, a version seems to have been popular in which the crossed members were in the shape of ducks' necks, heads and bills.

Tables were small and low. Dining took place at portable multi-purpose tables and wooden and reed examples survive. Storage chests were made for specific purposes, fitted out to contain wigs or toilet sets, as well as for general use. Painting and inlay were both used on them for decoration. Stands for pots were made with elegantly curved and splayed legs.

From the 18th dynasty onwards table and stool legs can be found which look as though they may have been turned but there is no proof that the Egyptians knew the use of the lathe until late in their history. It is likely that this tool was developed first by the civilizations which grew up between the Tigris and the Euphrates, and was then imported into Egypt.

Mesopotamia

Between c3500 BC and c500 BC a series of civilizations rose and collapsed by the Tigris and the Euphrates. In considering furniture a continuity can be seen between these civilizations except for a period of c500 years at the beginning of the Assyrian era (c1350–850 BC), from which time remains and representations of furniture are non-existent.

Damp and time have destroyed all but a few fragments of wooden furniture in Mesopotamia. Knowledge rests on the evidence of wall reliefs, ivory and bronze decorations, and cylinder seals. The extreme smallness of these seals makes it difficult to be sure of detail, but they provide the best, and for much of the time, the only evidence about the nature of the furniture of the Proto-Historic, Old Sumerian and Old Akkadian periods (c3500–2230 BC). From them it seems that box and framed stools and framed tables were in use very early; cross-legged and lattice stools appear by or before the Old Akkadian period (c2370–2230 BC). Sculpture introduces us to reed stools and to thrones decorated with carved lions at the side. A little later chairs with curved backs and cushions and stools with woven rush seats appear.

ANCIENT FURNITURE

Knowledge of the furniture of Assyrian and Neo-Babylonian times (1350–539 BC) is confined to palace furniture. Reliefs from the palaces of the 9th to the 7th centuries BC show tables with crossed legs and animal feet, thrones with high backs and stretchers, footstools and couches and the use of a pierced decoration of human figures upholding the arms of chairs of state. A common feature of this furniture is the use of feet shaped like cedar cones either alone or as supports for animal feet. This is reminiscent of the way in which the Egyptians used beaded cylinder supports, though there is no firm evidence of a connection. In the 8th and 7th centuries BC decoration was sometimes provided by ivory plaques incised with patterns of men and animals. Turning seems to have become common in Assyria,

Left: Assurbanipal and his wife are depicted feasting in a garden on this Assyrian relief, which is dated 668–627 BC. Much of the furniture, including his couch, her chair, the table and the Queen's footstool, has the cone-shaped feet of a lot of Assyrian and Babylonian furniture. From other reliefs of the period it looks as though the strange hybrid of lions' paws above cone-shaped feet was often used.

Right: a copy of the throne of Minos. The original in Crete is the oldest throne in Europe, dating from the Late Bronze Age. The wave-like pattern of the back suggests the Minoan rule of the sea. The detail of the sides makes it look as though the throne was made to resemble a wooden original: there is no constructional reason for indicating a stretcher in stone.

Babylonia and Egypt in the 7th century BC and to have spread to Greece at the same time.

Fine furniture was highly prized by the Assyrians: the prophet Nahum, celebrating the sack of Nineveh by the Medes in 612 BC, declared, "Take the spoil of silver, take the spoil of gold! There is no end to the treasure, the wealth of all manner of fine furniture."

Greece

Evidence of the furniture used in the earliest Greek civilizations, those of Minoan Crete and of Mycenae, is

so slight as to preclude forming any sort of picture of contemporary interiors. The so-called throne of Minos, from Knossos, is made of gypsum but looks as though it is based on a wooden model, indicating that wood was used for furniture construction. From Mycenae there are scraps of carved ivory mounts and plaques used as decoration on furniture. From other Mycenaean centers pottery representations of chairs with rounded, one-piece seats and backs remain whose construction can only be guessed. For the main body to have been made of wood appears impossible prior to the invention of steam pressing and laminated boards: the most likely material would be reeds or cane. At Pylos, a Mycenaean center, clay tablets have been found which list a number of items of furniture made of ebony, stone, yew wood and crystal, decorated with ivory and gold.

From c12th century BC, when Greece was overrun by the Dorians, to c700 BC there is no evidence of the

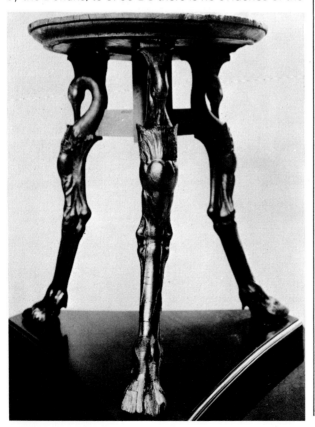

A three-legged Hellenistic stool found in Egypt, the only piece of Hellenistic furniture to survive almost intact. Animal forms for furniture legs were common throughout the Ancient world, but the complex mixture of anthropomorphic motifs on this stool stands in contrast to the simple bull or lion legs of earlier Egyptian furniture.

A 5th-century BC Greek vase depicting Terpsichore sitting on a *klismos*. The saber-shaped legs and curved back splat strongly influenced English Regency and French First Empire styles in the early 19th century.

furniture in use except for incidental mentions of furniture in the *Iliad* and the *Odyssey* which reached their final form at the end of the period.

A substantial amount of information about furniture from the Archaic period (mid-7th century–475 BC) survives in the form of terracotta models, sculpture and, above all, vase paintings. The couch or *kline* was used for sleeping and, by men, for reclining during meals. Women used chairs at meal times. The couch supports were sometimes turned, with a heavy, concave bell-shape at the top of the leg. This style is rather ugly and was soon replaced in popularity by rectangular legs decorated with palmettes and ovals, often with the ovals cut out to leave only a thin neck of wood supporting the bed. A pair of volutes often surmounted the legs at the bed head to raise it above the level of the foot. The mattress rested on leather strips or a criss-cross of cords attached to the frame.

The tables used for dining were small and could be placed under the couches when not in use. From vase paintings it seems that the most popular form of table was rectangular, with two legs at one end and one at the other and a bracket attached to the single leg to give stability to the top.

From illustrations it is clear that many types of stools and chairs existed. The *thronos* was a formal chair, with or without arms. It normally had rectangular legs decorated like those of a couch. Ordinary chairs and stools often stood on either turned or anthropomorphic legs with bull and lion legs the most common forms. Unlike Egyptian furniture, it is very rare to find the hind legs represented, even if the back legs of the chair are in animal form. Some cross-legged stools had animal feet arranged so that the front of the feet face each other, giving the stools an odd, knock-kneed appearance.

Chests were used for storage but many household articles were simply hung on nails on the wall.

The same types of furniture continued into the Classical and Hellenistic periods (after 475 BC). The only extant piece of Greek wooden furniture that is complete is a Hellenistic, three-legged table, found at Thebes in Egypt. It has a round top and the legs are in the form of swans' necks resting on goats' hooves. It may have originated in Greece or have been made by Greek workmen in Egypt. After the death of Alexander the Great two of his generals, Ptolemy and Seleucus became sovereigns of Egypt and Western Asia respectively, and Hellenistic designs became the common currency of the known world.

The two most important designs of Classical Greece for the long-term development of European furniture were the addition of curved, reclining head- and footboards to the couch and the creation of the *klismos* chair. This had saber legs at the front and at the rear. The curve of the front legs was continued and reversed in the posts supporting the back, which was formed of a curved, horizontal piece of wood at the height of the shoulder blades. It was arguably the most elegant shape ever created for a piece of seat furniture. Together with the Classical development of the couch it forms the basis of the lovely seat furniture of Regency England and Directory France.

A bronze stool of the 1st century AD. The concave seat rests on a frieze pierced with a pattern derived from a Greek design. A cushion would have been used on it. Bronze furniture was popular in the Roman world, though the price of the material would have made it available only to the richer classes of society.

Classical Greece saw the beginnings of baby furniture. The Egyptians had made children's chairs as miniatures of adult furniture since the child was regarded as a miniature adult. (A small-scale throne which was presumably used by Tutankhamun as a child was found in his tomb.) The Greeks seem to have looked at the jobs done by furniture and the needs of the child with the same clear-eyed pragmatism which Aristotle applied to philosophy. By the mid-5th century BC they had invented a baby chair which held the child securely and would be almost impossible for him to tip over unaided.

Etruria and Rome
The Etruscans inhabited Italy between the Arno and the Tiber and their civilization reached its apogee in the 7th century BC. It was in violent contact with the Greek colonizers of Southern Italy and became absorbed by Rome during the 2nd and 1st centuries AD.

ANCIENT FURNITURE

Contact with the Greeks however, was not all in the form of warfare. From the 6th century onwards the Greek couch was used by both men and women for eating and sleeping, but during the Hellenistic period women adopted the Greek habit of sitting on chairs for meals. Couches, which gained thicker mattresses and a head-board, were more comfortable than their Greek prototypes. Stools with turned legs, foot-stools with claw feet, thrones with bronze plaques overlaid on wood and three-legged rectangular tables were used, and in the 4th century BC the Etruscans adopted the Greek circular tripod table with anthropomorphic legs.

At Cerveteri, a town near Rome, a 3rd-century BC tomb known as the Tomb of the Reliefs yields a remarkable picture of an Etruscan house. The tomb is constructed like a living-room and the family's belongings are reproduced in stone and painted plaster. Couches are set by the walls, as is a replica of a clothes chest. Most of the family's goods are hung on nails and it is clear that container furniture was rare by modern standards.

In Rome, as in Etruria, it was not the custom to over-furnish houses but in the Imperial period it was fashionable to lavish money on the materials from which furnishings were made. Wooden furniture has decayed but a large enough number of marble and metal pieces remains to testify to the general use of marble, iron and bronze, at least among the well-to-do.

The most important piece of Roman furniture was the couch (*lectus*). It had the same dual use as among the Greeks and Etruscans and could be single or double. If double it was known as the *lectus genialis* or "marriage bed". In dining rooms couches were placed around three sides of a square and known corporately as *triclinia*. Although couches were usually made of oak or maple, exotic woods were also employed. Bronze was not uncommon, sometimes nielloed with gold or silver.

Massive marble side tables were introduced by the Romans but dining tables remained small and individual, following Greek models. Precious woods, metals and stones, tortoiseshell and ivory were lavished on them. Seneca is said to have given an enormous sum of money for an inlaid table of thuya or citron wood. The Hildesheim treasure, now in Berlin, contains a circular tripod table of the 1st century AD made of silver.

Motifs from the Ancient world: from the top, acanthus, egg and dart, ram's head, Roman fasces.

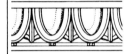

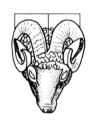

A bronze double seat depicted on a Roman fresco from Herculaneum. The legs, thick at the top and spindly below, have a Greek ancestry. The small winged creatures which support the arm derive from Egypt's sphinx.

Storage furniture still consisted mainly of chests. In addition the Romans produced the buffet or open cupboard. Silver and glass were immensely popular and buffets were introduced as a means of displaying precious vessels to their best advantage.

The most common forms of seat furniture were benches (*scamna*) and stools (*subsellia*). Backless folding stools, called *sellae*, were particularly popular. They could be of wood, iron or bronze. Magistrates had an ivory version and Julius Caesar, who, like most Romans, was not averse to display, had a gold *sella*.

ANCIENT FURNITURE

Chairs were uncommon. The grandest, the *thronus*, was reserved for divinities. The *cathedra*, an armchair with either a straight or sloping back, was used by women or by specially honored men, including religious and scholastic dignitaries.

Half-way between a seat and a bed was a couch which the Romans developed with a high back and sides lashed together at the top. The House of the Carbonized Furniture in Herculaneum contained one example.

The Romans of the Imperial age loved grandeur as the remains of their buildings make clear. The size of most sorts of furniture, however, is severely restricted by function. A chair or table too high for use is merely absurd. Some fringe forms of furniture, where functional demands were not so precise, became colossal. From Hadrian's villa at Tivoli marble candelabra remain which are considerably taller than a man.

Until the examination of Greek remains at the end of the 18th century European Classicism in the visual arts, including furniture making and interior decoration, meant Roman Classicism. Rome produced the motifs which were used throughout Western Europe from the Renaissance onwards. These were both modified Greek designs and their own creations. The fasces were specifically Roman. Originally from Greece, or even in some cases from Egypt and the Eastern Mediterranean, but filtered through Rome and applied for half a millennium to anything from a palace to a paper-weight, were trophies of war, acanthus leaves, paterae (oval rosettes), festoons of laurel or grapes, egg and dart, egg and tongue, the ram's head, sphinx, lion and eagle, the grotesque and the human mask. Despite the great debasement of the Dark Ages when motifs were either lost or deformed by bad craftsmanship and the alternative tradition of the Gothic period these motifs represent, albeit superficially, the dominant tradition of European expression.

Inlays of bone, ivory and semi-precious stones were frequently used on fine Egyptian furniture.

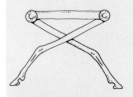

In Greece animal legs continued in use for folding stools, chairs and for circular tables.

ANCIENT FURNITURE

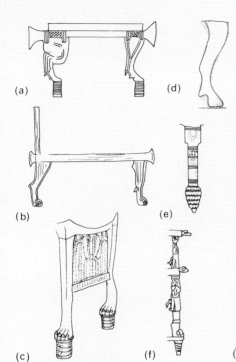

In Egypt technically fine furniture was being produced by 3000 BC alongside more primitive work. Before the 7th century BC, however, furniture contains no turned members. About that time the lathe was introduced from Mesopotamia and appeared in Greece too. The arts of gilding, painting and inlay appear frequently in Egyptian furniture. Mesopotamia produced excellent turned work but also adopted some Egyptian motifs and styles. Greek work was elegant rather than magnificent; the Roman Empire added its love of luxury to the Greek motifs which it employed.

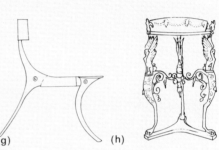

In Egypt animal legs decorated the front and back of couches and chairs. (a, b, c) In Sumeria only the front legs were animal (d); the back legs were straight. Assyrians preferred turned legs supported on pine cones (e) but lion feet were sometimes included in the complex decoration of the legs of offertory tables(f). In Greece anthropomorphism gave way to the elegant curves of the klismos (g). Rome readopted the animal leg but combined it with other forms (h).

By the 16th century BC lattice design stools in Egypt were common, sometimes with a concave seat, sometimes with a double cave seat. The seat could be solid wood or woven reeds.

Folding stools with ducks-neck legs and leather seats were popular in Egypt.

ORIENTAL FURNITURE

The furniture of China, Korea, Japan, India and the Islamic countries is very different to that found in the West. Few equivalents exist. Beauty was found in bare rooms, and luxury in carpets.

China and Korea

Chinese furniture developed from two basic forms of construction: the box and the rack. By the early Chou period (c1000 BC) box construction was in use, as can be seen from an extant bronze table which imitates a wooden frame and panel construction. The method of box construction, however, differs from that now common in the West. Nearly all Chinese furniture depended on the mortise and tenon principle; dovetailing was sometimes used but far less often than in Europe; doweling was only used for repairs; nails were never employed and glue was used only very sparingly. The reasons for these details of construction are twofold; through much of China temperatures change dramatically between day and night and large areas of the country are humid. An unglued tenon and mortise joint can be made loose enough to expand without splitting the wood and yet not appear unsightly. This is not true of dovetail joints and nailed wood cannot move at all in the same way. Secondly, the Chinese maintained the habit, widespread in Europe in the Middle Ages, of traveling frequently from place to place and thus needed to be able to pack and move easily. Furniture was made, therefore, to be quickly dismantled. The exception to this is the massive palace furniture of the 17th to 19th centuries which was made for a specific setting.

The relationship of furniture to architecture was established early in China. The basic oriental sitting posture is not the same as in the West, with back and lower leg at right angles to the ground; nor are resting positions flat and reclining as they are in the West. Instead oriental people sit cross-legged or with one foot tucked under them, the other leg hanging down; or they recline, resting on one elbow. Both these postures can be taken up on the floor; they do not require chairs. The floor has rarely proved comfortable anywhere, and in China, to raise the body from the cold and possibly damp ground, a brick platform was built at one end of the room. In winter the platform could be heated through flues. This platform or *k'ang* served as a bed and as a seat, with the occupants sitting cross-legged

An 18th- or early 19th-century Chinese table. It is made of rosewood, and has the square legs often seen, though the break in them is unusual. The round ends of the table top are more complicated than usual, as is the carved decoration which appears on them and below the table top. The Chinese did not have specific dining rooms; tables like this one were carried in for the purpose.

on rush mats placed on its top. By 81 BC in at least some parts of China the *k'ang* had been supplemented by wooden beds with hangings and screens for privacy. Both beds and screens, together with embroidered cushions and felt or boarhide floor coverings were deplored by the conservative writer of a review of Chinese governmental expansionist policy. In this writer the Han dynasty (206 BC–221 AD) found its representative of that ageless tribe which sees any evidence of increased physical comfort as a harbinger of moral and social collapse.

The *k'ang* had become a wooden structure by 1000 BC; and it is possible to see a very clear line of development whereby the *k'ang* from being a seat-cum-bed, became a table. By a similar progression it continued to be a form of seating but developed into a wide sofa. The basic *k'ang* shape is that of a platform made up of four rostra set side by side. In the front of each rostrum in the early periods there were two rectangular cut-outs, one placed above the other. In the 8th century during the T'ang dynasty (618–906 AD) the four rostra were joined together and the cut-outs replaced by one large ogee-headed cut-out. By the 13th century, although

the bottom frame remained, the panel had disappeared and the four corners of the construction had become, in effect, legs which continue the line of the decorative arch and curve delicately inwards as they descend. At some time in the late 14th century, in the early Ming period (1368–1644), the bottom rail disappeared altogether and the inward sweeping legs were terminated in what became probably the most commonly employed motif in Chinese furniture, the horse hoof or *ma-t'i*. During the 18th century it was to be replaced by a rather sloppy scroll. The very low table was placed on the brick *k'ang*, where one existed, and stood on its own; those using it sat cross-legged on mats. Given a low back and sides of rack construction the *k'ang* became a low sofa. Woven matting covered the base or, in the grandest houses, a silk-covered cushion.

By the 4th century AD Buddhism had been successfully taken to China from India and with it the Chinese

A 12-fold Chinese screen, c1662–1722, made in lacquered wood, which is carved, painted and gilt, and decorated with fabulous beasts, birds, landscapes and seascapes. In front of it is a throne in black with gilding on it. The legs are a development of the *k'ang*.

acquired ideas from much further away than India. The conquests of Alexander the Great in Northern India in the 4th century had introduced Classical European ideas of furnishing to the sub-continent, including the use of the folding stool or chair. The Hellenistic influence was continued at a distance by trading contacts with Rome. The Buddhists took their Western-style seating arrangements to China and the Chinese slowly adapted them. At first they sat cross-legged on the stools but by the 9th century the European backed chair was in ordinary use, except amongst the poor, and it was used in the European manner. The seat, however, was higher than is now usual in the West since the chair was intended for use with a foot-stool. Armchairs were regarded as seats of honor and were usually reserved for men. In time China was to repay the debt to Europe by exporting the cabriole leg; this appeared in China in perhaps the 15th century, during the Ming period.

Until the 19th century thrones in China were not really chairs in the European sense. They were a development of the *k'ang*, and could be used with the occupant's legs tucked under his body. However, from illustrations it appears as if, at least on formal occasions, the Emperors sat in the customary European manner. Thrones were usually not of plain wood but were lacquered. Palace furniture on the whole was far more ornate than the furniture used outside the court. Lacquer was a great favorite. The rules of etiquette at the Court of Heaven extended even to the furnishings. By a decree of 1029 AD red lacquer beds were reserved for the Emperor. Among the non-Imperial rich the favorite color for this kind of bed seems to have been black.

Storage furniture was more highly developed by the 17th century than any other sort of furnishing. Cupboards were used for most articles other than clothes, which were stored in chests. In the T'ang period chests-on-chests appeared. As early as the Han period there were chests-on-stands. Nickel silver was popular for mounts in both China and Korea, whose patterns of development followed very closely on those of Northern China. In both countries chest furniture was rarely veneered, though there are extant examples of walnut being used as carcase wood with a rosewood veneer.

The favorite wood for furniture used by the Chinese

ORIENTAL FURNITURE

and Koreans alike was rosewood. The Chinese divide the rosewoods into a whole series of types of which the most highly prized was *lingoum santalinum*, a purple-black rosewood.

One element of joinery constantly used in the making of European furniture is lacking in China. The Chinese never invented a lathe. In consequence until the European domination of the late 19th century there was no turned work. The legs of many Chinese tables of the trestle type appear to be round in section but on examination prove to be less than exactly circular. They are carved from the block in precisely the same way as a conventional piece of sculpture.

The furniture of China and Korea shows none of the complex development and certainly none of the speed of change apparent in the history of Western furniture. In general, particularly with palace furnishings, the more ornate a piece is the later it is likely to be. This does not, however, obtain with lacquer screens, already highly decorated by the 17th century.

A Chinese chest dating from the early 15th century. It is made of polychrome filled-in lacquer, that is a lacquer filled in with the design. Storage furniture became highly developed in China, unlike other types of furniture.

A Korean sutra box of the lacquer known as *maki-e*. The design was made of tiny pieces of gold wire set into lacquer. Korean work derives from the Chinese but in this kind of lacquer, a Japanese speciality, the Koreans excelled. It was used mainly on small articles of furniture.

Japan

Japanese houses are even more austere than their Chinese counterparts and furniture consists of even fewer types. The basic furnishings of a Japanese house are the *tatami* mats which cover the floor, providing the major seating area of a room. Unlike China Japan never accepted Western seating habits in the home. Everything, consequently, is lower than its Western counterpart. Tables are only several inches high and, in common with much other Japanese furniture, have forked legs. They are often lacquered and inlaid. The same is true of writing desks, reading stands, cabinets and, a quintessentially Japanese form of furniture, the kimono stand. A kimono stand is usually beautifully decorated. Its shape has not changed since the 11th century. It resembles a towel rail, two thin uprights connected by three rods, one at the top, one at the bottom and one in the middle; it is an example of rack construction.

In general the forms of Chinese furniture were followed by the Japanese, except for seat furniture, but two specifically Japanese styles of storage furniture developed from their Chinese originals. The *kodansu* is a small cabinet which can take a number of forms. It is usually lacquered and inlaid and can have a number of open shelves or closed shelves and even drawers. Its construction is very light, consisting simply of rods joined together to enclose a small space and backed with a panel of light wood or parchment. The *karabitsu* (Chinese chest) is also small but is a more substantial piece of furniture. It is a small chest for domestic use on

63

A print by Mizuno
Toshikata, carried out
c1890–1900,
depicting a Japanese
tea ceremony.
Japanese houses
contained very little
furniture. Ideally, a
room was furnished
with mats and nothing
else, the focus being
the alcove (*tokonama*)
with one object of
beauty placed in front
of it for contemplation.
Here the alcove has a
hanging scroll with a
vase and flower
arrangement below it.

A 17th-century black lacquer three-tiered box on a stand from the Ryukyu islands. It is an example of "*lac burgauté*". Tiny slivers of mother-of-pearl, ranging in color from green and grey to pale violet, are set into the wet lacquer to give a shimmering effect to the landscape. Their delicate colors are emphasized by the solid black of the lacquer. The box is the same size as a chest-of-drawers.

short forked legs and in the Fujiwara period (898–1185 AD) it became usual to decorate it with landscapes and with *maki-e* (spray painting with gold dust).

Although they had few types of furniture the Japanese developed the decoration of furniture to a fine art. Some of the finest artists painted screens, both the one-leaf *tsuitate* and the several-leaved *byobu* and the best Japanese lacquer is probably superior to that of China. Besides *maki-e* Japan perfected *kin-gin-e* or lacquer painted with gold and silver and *roden*, the application of a mother-of-pearl inlay, which, in the form of *lac burgauté* was exported as a technique from Japan to the Ryukyu islands where some of the loveliest examples now extant were made.

In the main the Japanese home has changed little in design for many centuries. By Western standards the *tatami* mats, the hanging scroll and the few pieces of furniture may present an austere appearance. They also, however, represent stability in the middle of flux. Japanese society has undergone rapid changes in the last 100 years whereas her furniture has scarcely changed since the Asoka period (552–710 AD).

India and Islam

Most Islamic countries retained into modern times the common Asiatic posture of sitting cross-legged. Through most of the Islamic world furniture meant carpets, fine fabrics and cushions. In India, wooden furniture of one sort of another has certainly been constructed for millennia; but nothing remains of any early furniture because of the climate and the ravages of insect life. Clothes chests of the 17th and 18th centuries AD survive, because, to protect their contents, the chests were made of brass laid over teak.

Before the Moslem conquest of the 8th century India possessed beds, small tables known as *chanki* which may have doubled as stools, folding chairs and wicker chairs. The beds followed the Egyptian and Babylonian models, with short carved legs which were either of lacquered, painted or gilded wood, carved from ivory or, in some luxurious cases, cast in silver. Under the Moslems a more massive, European-looking bed was introduced and under British rule, which effectively began in the 18th century, the four-poster became popular. Given the limited range of furniture used, beds quite often doubled as sofas.

As in China the wide sofa also developed into a throne. The frame was often overlaid with beaten gold plates and sometimes encrusted with precious stones. In the 16th century the Moslems introduced the Asiatic throne which was raised up with a short flight of steps and a rectangular or octagonal seating platform. It was provided with a back and sides; the earlier couch-cum-throne had gained a back in the 8th century. At some time during the 14th or 15th century the custom developed of placing a canopy in the shape of a sunshade over the throne.

The chair had been introduced to India by the Hellenistic kingdom left behind by Alexander the Great in the 4th century BC but it only became other than a seat of honor with the European conquests of the 18th century. European models were then copied in ivory, silver and even gold. From time to time in the 18th century small tables were also made of silver. Naturally most of the furniture made in precious metals has since disappeared into the melting pot.

Of storage furniture very little survives. Of all Islamic furnishings it is carpets into which most work was put. It is they, not furniture in the conventional sense, which dictated the appearance of the Islamic interior.

EARLY EUROPEAN FURNITURE

From the 3rd to the 15th century furniture ceased to be a much-used commodity. However, the fine craftsmanship that was applied to architecture was also applied to furniture, as were the motifs and styles.

In 284 AD the Emperor Diocletian divided the Roman world in two: the Western Empire, centered on Rome, and the Eastern Empire, whose capital was Byzantium. In the 5th century Rome was sacked three times, after which the Eastern Empire became the major repository of Roman styles. Our information about furniture in Europe for the next 900 years is scanty; it comes from manuscript illuminations, literature and the rare pieces of furniture that survive.

The *Vienna Genesis*, a manuscript from the Eastern Empire which was probably written in the 6th century, shows examples of turned stools with X stretchers, a bed or bench with turned legs, a table with X stretchers and a throne-like basketwork chair with a high back which forms a surround for the shoulders of the occupant (in this case Jacob) and a canopy for his head. This piece is particularly interesting since it can be traced in pictures from the 3rd to the 12th century and from one end of Europe to the other. A Romano-British monument at York of the late 2nd or early 3rd century AD depicts such a chair.

Although the furniture of the Byzantine Empire was more sophisticated than that made in most of the Western Empire, particularly in its use of inlay, workmanship of a high order can be found at times in small areas of Western Europe, particularly where a strong ruler

An illustration from the 6th-century *Vienna Genesis*, showing one kind of chair seen all over Medieval Europe. The picture reveals the chair as a symbol of authority. Jacob's feet rest on a dais—the precursor of the footstool—which was a separate piece of furniture.

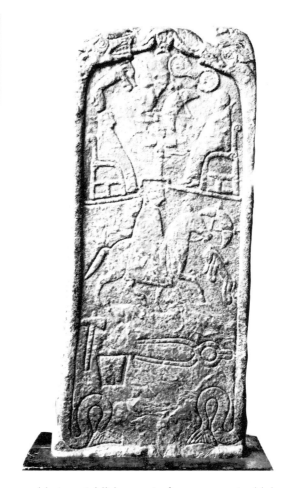

A 7th-century Pictish symbol stone from Dunfallandy in Scotland. The horse and chair are both ancient symbols of authority. Each chair is supported on a podium. The design of the chairs shows that the originals were made of wood, since the cross members holding the chair together would not have been necessary in stone. The seat is beveled and the chair backs are scroll-topped.

was able to establish a seat of government which appeared, at least temporarily, to be stable. The so-called Chair of Dagobert, an example of 7th-century Frankish workmanship, is an excellent reworking of the Roman curule or magistrate's chair in gilt bronze. Even in places far removed from the centers of civilization, for example in 7th-century Scotland, there is evidence that aesthetic considerations affected furniture making. A mini Classical revival began in Europe under Charlemagne; he had furniture plated with precious metals in imitation of the Caesars. As a further Roman touch the round-headed or Romanesque arch was employed both structurally in buildings and as a decorative motif on furniture. This was not a purely Western phenomenon. The St Matthew illumination in the *Codex Ebnerianus*, a Byzantine manuscript of the 12th century, shows the apostle seated in a chair decorated with just such arches.

Life in the Middle Ages was unstable and, so far as comfort is concerned, frugal. The peasantry owned little furniture other than objects roughly knocked together by each household for its own use. The aristocracy, by modern standards, lived a life lacking in amenity. Kings and great barons were regularly on the move from one residence to another which meant that most furnishings had to be easily transportable. Chests were strong, and in the days before joined chests became common this also meant heavy, but they were usually suitable for loading on carts. Tables were normally boards with separate trestles, although *dormant* or fixed tables are sometimes referred to in Medieval literature. The normal forms of seat furnishing were the bench, stool and settle. The chair was reserved as a sign of authority and was X shaped, sometimes folding, sometimes fixed, or was a square, throne-like structure.

By far the most important element in furnishing was fabric: curtains to exclude draughts, wall hangings and covers. Until as late as the 17th century descriptions of beds concentrate on the hangings to the exclusion of the woodwork, which usually merely provided a frame. For many the bench formed the base of a bed, and more elaborate beds, built on the box principle, served as seats during the day.

The box bed was one of the longest lasting forms of furniture. A 12th-century sculpture of the Virgin at Chartres shows her lying in a box bed which has a useful gap in the middle of the front to ease entry and exit. In 1891 the writer Jerome K. Jerome had problems getting into a box bed in a provincial German inn. Sometimes the bed would be divided from the main part of the room by a curtain or a rail and sometimes the bed itself would have curtains suspended from a canopy attached to the ceiling.

A second type of bed which appeared in the Middle Ages and enjoyed a long use was the built-in or cupboard bed. This was often completely enclosed, with access through a door. At a time when privacy was difficult to obtain and most rooms were multi-purpose its advantages are clear. Such beds can still be found in Scandinavia; an 18th-century version exists at Balderston in Yorkshire.

A 15th-century Arras tapestry entitled *l'Offrande du coeur*, in which a gentleman offers a lady his heart. The setting of a wood is unusual; such scenes were more often placed in an enclosed garden. Tapestries were much appreciated by the wealthy since they provided warmth and were an easily movable form of furnishing. The couple are courtly—the lady has a hawk on her hand, evidence of an aristocratic pastime.

In Western Europe the Romanesque style gradually gave way to the Gothic in the late 12th and the 13th centuries. The round-headed arch was superseded by the pointed arch. Both these architectural styles were reflected in furniture. In Italy the Gothic maintained an uneasy truce with the Romanesque and had comparatively little influence on design except in the North. Throughout most of Italy a barbarized Classicism continued to be the dominant style: very little remains from this period. Further North in what is now Russia the

71

successive devastations of Bulgars, Cumans, Alans and Mongols ensured that until the late 15th century so much effort was needed merely to stay alive that the graces of living hardly arose. At the other end of Europe Spain had been conquered by the Moors in 711 AD. Since the Christian kingdoms did not repel the invader until 1492 the Gothic style in Spain took on a pronouncedly Eastern tinge, with Moorish forms of decoration within Gothic shapes.

Medieval Europe was a continent under siege, torn by violent internal conflicts. There was insufficient sense of permanence and leisure, nor was there the specialization of work to produce new functions to meet which new forms of furniture would have been evolved. The jobs which furniture was required to do were no more sophisticated in the 15th century than they had been in the 8th century. Only minor developments took place: as joiners became more skilled chests became lighter. In Northern Europe the aumbry or livery cupboard was created, probably to hold food. It was an enclosed version of the true cupboard which consisted of a shelf or series of shelves left open and used for the display of drinking vessels and plate. The aumbry was sufficiently enclosed to hide its contents

A late 15th-century French chest of carved oak, showing the enormous influence of Gothic architecture on furniture. At the corners, sides and on the front are Gothic pinnacles derived from the form of architectural buttresses. Here they serve a purely decorative function. The use of blind tracery in the panels is copied from 15th-century window tracery.

The Coronation Chair from Westminster Abbey, England. It was made for King Edward I, in or soon after 1296. Made out of oak, the Gothic architectural derivation of its arcading, gabling and pinnacles is clear. The supporting lions were added in 1727 to replace lions which were themselves added in 1509.

but had decorative pierced carving to allow a free flow of air around the food. From the late 12th century in some ecclesiastical houses presses in which clothes could be hung or laid flat began to replace chests. The most spectacular of these are great semi-circular presses for copes.

Although there was no great change in the types of furniture in use decoration altered considerably. The

EARLY EUROPE

Gothic style of architecture came to dominate all the arts and architectural motifs were adopted by carpenters and joiners. Wainscotting, lining walls with wooden panels and frames, had led to enclosed beds and chairs with paneled box seats and in-filled backs and arms. In the 15th and 16th centuries Flemish and English linenfold decoration on wall paneling was echoed on chests and chairs. From the 13th century onwards Gothic arcading, buttressing and window tracery, structurally important in buildings, were applied decoratively to furnishings and as the Gothic style changed in architecture so those changes are mirrored in furniture. It is usually only by the style of decoration that any attempt can be made to date pieces of Medieval furniture, and then only if the country of origin is known. Techniques of decoration are not a lot of help in dating. Chip carving was common in the 13th century but it can still be found even in Italy, the most artistically advanced of European countries, in the 15th century. Turned decoration was in use throughout the Medieval period. Fine inlays, however, suggest a late date—c15th century—for any piece on which they appear.

In the 13th century there was a rapid growth of the most important secular literary motif of the Middle Ages: the Arthurian legends, to which were annexed the legends of Troy and of Charlemagne, all of them lauding a code of chivalry and courtesy and joining with saints' lives to produce a powerful hybrid. Especially in England, France and Germany incidents from the legends appear again and again on chests and mirror backs and they are one of the most common sources of illustration on the misericord seats of the English cathedrals.

In the Middle Ages the work of goldsmiths and jewelers was particularly highly esteemed. Gold was easily portable wealth, and in lean times it went into the pot to emerge as bullion. Fabrics were portable wealth of a different kind. They provided a minimum comfort, and the most attractive furnishings of the Middle Ages are their tapestries. The series of The Lady with the Unicorn in the Cluny Museum in Paris has all the grace and delicacy and the completely artificial charm of an Arthurian decadence, but even here the wooden furniture depicted—a Gothic stool—despite its brocade cushion, is a reminder of the actual spartan world whose conditions the tapestry was produced to alleviate.

Turning was the usual technique of chair making from Scandinavia to Italy by the 12th century.

Gothic element developed in chip-carved roundels of the late 13th century.

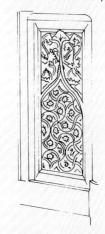

Gothic window tracery was copied on carved decoration for chest panels.

EARLY EUROPE

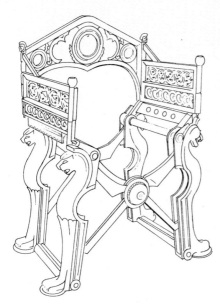

Classical art survived in Byzantium until its fall in the 15th century. In Western Europe by the 9th century the court of Charlemagne resurrected Classical motifs for court furniture. The main influences on furniture making throughout Europe derived from turning, the basic technique of chair making, and from contemporary architecture. The forms of Romanesque and Gothic architecture occur in turn on furniture. Oak was the wood most frequently used, though fruitwoods and chestnut were popular in Spain.

Lion monopodia copied from Roman originals were used by Carolingian bronze-casters for royal chairs.

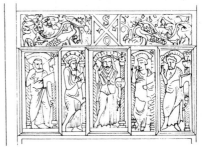

Byzantine 6th century ivory workers combined Classically draped Christian figures with patterns of vines and animals, scenes from the life of Christ and the Chi Ro Monogram.

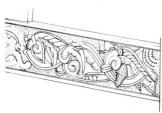

In Norway powerful, harsh forms are close to Viking origins.

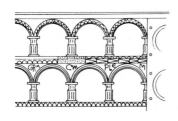

Blind arcading of round-headed arches copied on furniture from arcades in Romanesque churches. 13th century.

Gothic arcading, pinnacles and gables were added to thrones.

FROM THE RENAISSANCE TO 1800

Since the Renaissance began in Italy her furniture shows its impact a century before the rest of Europe. However, the political and cultural cross-currents between Spain, the Netherlands and the German and Italian states justify treating these countries together. In 1519 Charles V was elected Holy Roman Emperor, after which time most of these areas formed for a while a single political unit. Even after political ties were loosened cultural cross-currents continued to operate.

Italy

The city states of Italy developed during the Middle Ages as a response of both barbarian conquerors and native inhabitants to the problem of administering the peninsula. Groups of these states formed alliances against invasion from France, The Holy Roman Empire, and Spain. Others supported the invader. As a result there was a complicated see-saw of power. Of the many states existing by the 15th century those which were to develop distinctive styles of furniture making were Venice, Florence, Milan, Genoa, Rome (in the Papal States) and Sicily.

General poverty was widespread, and in some states, of which the Papal States and Sicily were glaring examples, continued to be remarked by foreign visitors until as late as the 19th century. Little furniture was made for the poor, and none remains. Such Re-

A sumptuous *cassone*, one of a pair made in 1472 for a marriage between members of the Nerli and Morelli families in Florence. It is a typical sarcophagus *cassone* with lions' feet echoing a Classical form. Made of gilded wood, the crisp carving makes it a very fine piece. On the left is the coat-of-arms of the Nerli family; the arms of the Morelli family are on the opposite side. The painted scenes are from Roman history and make allusions to the contemporary families. At this time some of the foremost painters in Italy were commissioned to decorate *cassone*.

naissance furniture as now exists was made for the great princes and magnates. Extant furniture of as late a date as the 18th century is furniture made for a much smaller middle class than that in most of Western Europe or North America; more usually it was made for members of the sizable aristocracy.

The Renaissance examination of Roman antiquities and use of their motifs was not for a purely archeological end, but was a search for modes of expression to articulate contemporary ideas.

There are two reasons why Renaissance furniture was significantly different from that of the Romans: the paucity of models before the excavation of Pompeii and Herculaneum was begun in the 18th century and the enormous differences between the society of the Julians and Claudians and that of the Sforza, the Medici and the Borgias.

Life for Renaissance princes and magnates was primarily distinguished from that of their Medieval predecessors in being a more settled affair. Unlike feudal lords, Renaissance rulers were not constantly on the move, and consequently their furniture could remain in one place. However, throughout the 15th and early 16th centuries great houses in most of Italy retained at least some of the aspects of mini fortresses against the danger of civil strife. Only in Venice was a less forbidding aspect possible. Inside the courtyard, however, a lighter arrangement of colonnades brought an element of graciousness to the interior: this was a development seen throughout Italy.

There was no return to the openness of the Roman villa and no return to its comfortable central heating. Whereas Roman rooms allowed a flexible disposition of furniture, Renaissance rooms were normally dominated by the fireplace just as Medieval halls had been, and any fixed seat furniture was arranged with regard to the fire and to the light source. Fixed window seats continued to be made, as can be seen from 15th- and 16th-century paintings. Storage furniture was often built into the walls. Some free-standing furniture was so heavy that it was practically fixed. The *cassone* or chest was sometimes given a back and arms and transformed into a chest/bench called a *casapanca*, which stood massively against the wall.

Renaissance design was developed in Florence, from which city ideas traveled rapidly throughout Italy. The most typical piece of furniture was still the *cassone*

and highly sophisticated Renaissance versions can be found from most parts of the peninsula. The method of construction varied according to the taste and wealth of the purchaser. Sometimes pieces of walnut or Spanish chestnut were used which were large enough to form the whole side of a chest and deep enough to allow carving in high relief. The motifs were usually mythological, with sirens or satyrs as corner embellishments; coats of arms were regularly incorporated and gadrooning (ornamental notching or carving) was very common around the bottom of the box and the edge of the lid. Alternatively a paneled construction was sometimes used in which a geometrical decoration would be inlaid or shallowly carved. Sometimes the inlaid or carved sections were applied to a joined chest. The third method was to cover a planked carcase with parchment or gesso which was then carved, gilded and painted. The motifs mentioned were not exclusive to any one type of construction. The simplest *cassone* rested directly on the floor, but many had feet shaped like lions' paws, which was a reversion to a Classical motif. A further debt to Rome was the frequent adoption of the sarcophagus shape, which seems an inappropriate choice since pairs of *cassone* were often presented as part of a marriage settlement.

Cassone were decorated by some of the foremost painters of the Renaissance and, at least in Florence, workshops existed which were devoted entirely to this activity. A number of works painted on wood, now hanging in the galleries of Europe and America as easel pictures, once formed part of such chests. As the century progressed elaborate gilding and painting became less frequent, and polished, carved panels in high relief were preferred.

A 16th-century Florentine *casapanca*, which combines the functions of a *cassone* and a sofa. About twelve feet in length, it was clearly made to stand by the wall in a palatial house. Architectural influence is apparent in the large volutes at the front. The piece has a Classical simplicity which adds to its grandeur. The front has simple carving on it.

These chairs are derived from the Roman curule chair

Top: The Chair of Dagobert, in gilt bronze. The back is not original, being probably a 12th-century addition. The rest of the chair is 7th century. The four lion monopodia copy the Classical form.

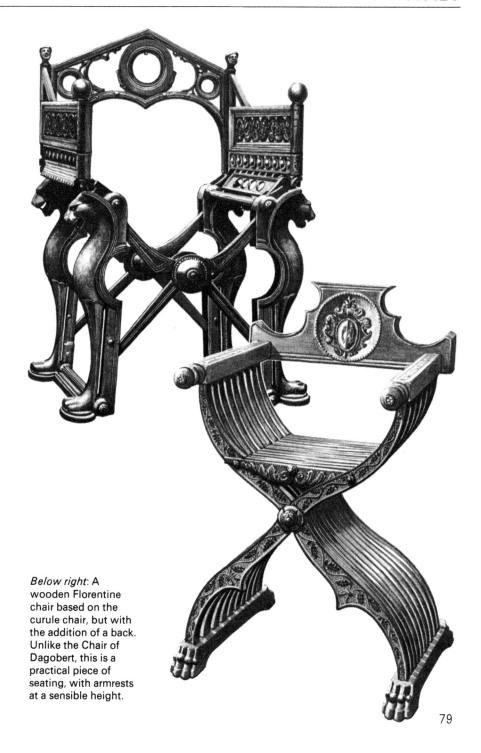

Below right: A wooden Florentine chair based on the curule chair, but with the addition of a back. Unlike the Chair of Dagobert, this is a practical piece of seating, with armrests at a sensible height.

RENAISSANCE

The Roman curule chair, which had never completely disappeared in Europe, was developed to a new level of elegance in the 15th and 16th centuries. A back was now added and the whole chair was usually made in wood, though metal versions of the backless variety were still used. These might be in bronze, iron or a combination of metals. The use of chairs instead of stools and benches seems to have increased in well-to-do Italian houses during the 16th century. Cane-seated

A 16th-century Venetian chair, whose shape is probably the most common form of the time. Such chairs were made in sets and placed in halls or in the main reception rooms of Venetian palaces. They were not very comfortable. The mask on the back and on the front below the seat was a common motif, as was the trailing vine.

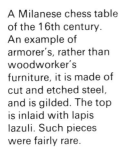

A Milanese chess table of the 16th century. An example of armorer's, rather than woodworker's furniture, it is made of cut and etched steel, and is gilded. The top is inlaid with lapis lazuli. Such pieces were fairly rare.

ladder back chairs were common and to a lesser extent so were armchairs with fabric-covered seats and backs, the fabric being joined to the wooden frame with decorative brass-headed nails. Sets of high-backed chairs were produced for ante-rooms which show a livelier sense of decoration than of comfort.

Tables were made in marble for some of the more magnificent palaces. These had a sense of weight and grandeur drawn directly from ancient Rome. Writing tables were still produced, as they had been in the Middle Ages. No specialized dining table or dining room existed and portable tables would be set up in any room in the house, wherever the owner felt like eating. Some of the most attractive pieces of furniture that remain are the small "fancy" pieces, made not by woodworkers but by armorers. Milan was a center for this sort of work which involved setting metal (and sometimes stone) inlays into engraved metal.

The most spectacular development in 16th-century Italy was the use of inlays of semi-precious stones and marble to form table tops and door panels. The fashion probably began in Milan. It was encouraged when the Grand Duke Ferdinand de'Medici formed the *Opificio delle Pietre Dure* in Florence in 1599. This was a study center and workshop for the production of goods in semi-precious stones. The stone used in furniture could be flat or set in high relief; the repertory of motifs included fruit, flowers and landscapes.

From the 15th century Classical ornament such as columns, acanthus leaves, scrolls and human figures was regularly employed on all forms of furniture, except for beds. These remained a matter of a simple wooden structure hidden by fine fabrics until late in the 16th century and in many places well beyond. More complicated beds with carved corner posts appear in a number of paintings of the period but none have survived.

Keeping pace with the development of Mannerism in the fine arts, decoration in the 16th century often became over-elaborate and confused, even in Tuscany, although the restraint of Florentine tradition did ensure the continued production of a few well proportioned buffets and cupboards.

In 1509 part of Nero's Golden House was excavated in Rome. The surviving decorations were seen by the painter Raphael who designed frescoes for the Vatican loggia in the same style. They consisted of mythical creatures and human figures surrounded by swags of leaves, fruit and flowers. Because the Golden House decorations were below ground level they were called "grotesques" and under that name they were to become a dominant motif of furniture and of interior decoration through much of Europe for three centuries.

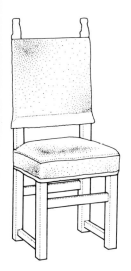

In the late 16th and early 17th centuries there were great changes in Europe in almost all branches of the arts and sciences. In the ordinary comforts of life, however, there was little development. By the middle of the 17th century Italian houses were furnished much as they had been 100 years earlier. There were more chairs and heavily carved walnut cupboards and tables were more common, especially in the North, but textiles still played the most important part in providing a sense of comfort or luxury to interiors. By modern standards even the most luxurious interior would seem oddly bleak. Even in the early 18th century the average living room of a wealthy Italian family seems to have been a simply furnished apartment.

In architecture the Baroque age started c1600. Beginning in Italy, it was a style patronized at first by Popes and cardinals but the forms and way of thinking soon penetrated the whole of Europe, Protestant North as well as Catholic South. As a style it was designed to

Italian 16th-century walnut furniture, a stick chair, upright chair and a table.

A late 17th-century carved Florentine cabinet-on-stand by Leonardo van der Vinne, a Fleming who directed the Grand Ducal workshops in Florence. The supports are of bronze and are Italian in style; the use of floral motifs on the cabinet derives from the Low Countries. The veneer is of tortoiseshell, ivory and silver, with columns in ivory, gilt-bronze and *pietre dure*.

create an emotional appeal by its sumptuous beauty. Church interiors, for example, included numerous decorative sculptures and paintings, and a lavish use of gilt, stucco and richly colored marbles. Furniture design, however, lagged far behind the other arts. Cupboards, the most splendid early 17th-century objects, tended to retain a rectangularity which accorded little with the Herculean curves of Baroque design.

Baroque furniture began to appear from 1670 in the state rooms of Rome, Venice, Genoa, Florence and Turin, as the great new papal and mercantile families began to display their wealth and their taste. Baroque furniture in the grand manner is the product of the sculptor, not of the cabinet-maker or joiner. Indeed, by the standards of English or French cabinet-making of the 17th and 18th centuries the workmanship of almost all contemporary Italian furniture is intolerably shoddy.

BAROQUE

A vase stand by the Italian designer Brustolon, part of a set of furniture which he made for the Palazzo Venier in Venice between 1684 and 1696. The pieces resemble sculpture rather than furniture. This vase stand is of carved ebony and boxwood. The motif of the negro slave was a frequent one, used as a support for Venetian furniture in the late 17th and early 18th centuries. There are three dragons at the base.

Its virtues lie in superb materials and, even more, in vigorously executed sculpture. These virtues seem to have been first employed on side tables; a type of furniture which supplemented the *credenza* (a serving table or side-board) which had been in use since the Middle Ages. Side tables now became purely decorative.

Motifs associated with water were particularly popular in Baroque art, not only in Venice, which as trading center of the Adriatic and of the Eastern Mediterranean had absorbed the symbolism of the sea as her property for centuries, but also throughout Italy and much of Europe. Perhaps the rotundity of waves and the connection of water with fruitfulness were seen as peculiarly appropriate to so swelling a style. Whatever the reason Tritons, river gods, shells and sea-horses

A mid-18th-century chest-of-drawers of Italian *lacca*. The strongly *bombé* shape was very common for Italian chests through the first two-thirds of the 18th century, as was the painted decoration of flowers. Although the decoration is lively, the quality of the workmanship is not high. Italian craftsmanship of this time is inferior to French, German and English work. The bottom drawer does not fit well and the quality of the carving lacks crispness and finesse.

abound as supports and decorations in Baroque furniture.

In Florence *pietre dure* was used lavishly by Giovanni Battista Foggini; in Genoa Domenico Parodi produced fantasies in gilded wood and in Venice probably the finest of all Italian Baroque pieces came from the hand of Andrea Brustolon. Besides being an able sculptor Brustolon was a craftsman. His workmanship lifts his furniture far above the level of that of any other contemporary Italian furniture maker. So far as is known he worked mainly on ecclesiastical commissions in his native Belluno but for a period of 12 years in the 1680s and 1690s he was producing secular furniture in Venice. During this period he made a set of furniture for Pietro Venier. The quality of this work is outstanding when compared to other Baroque furniture. It consists of chairs, *guéridons* and a side-table. The arms, legs and structures of the upholstered boxwood chairs are in the form of creeper-entwined branches. The front arm supports are beautifully carved and lacquered in the shape of negroes. A side-table, whose only purpose is to carry a set of china vases, sports figures of two river gods, three negro slaves, Hercules,

Cerberus and the Hydra. It is suitable that Venice should be the place where the exotic, the fantastic and the exuberant in Baroque furniture combine, partly because of her past and partly because in the 18th century she continued to produce some of the most sumptuous Italian furniture at the moment when the Rococo style emerged from the Baroque, c1730.

It is equally fitting that the center for fashionable lacquer furniture in the 18th century should have been Venice because of her trade with the East. Oriental lacquer had been appreciated in Europe since the 16th century and occidental substitutes were in use in England, France and the German states by the end of the 17th century. Venetian lacquer is not of the same quality as the best produced in the North, but can be very attractive. The word *lacca* is used now, as it was then, to describe japanned and painted furniture. The japanning was usually thinner and even further from oriental lacquer than its Northern European counterpart but similar oriental motifs were popular. *Lacca contrefata* was a cheaper substitute made by sticking colored paper designs onto furniture and varnishing the whole. Painted furniture was particularly popular in Venice but was to be found even in a few fairly modest houses throughout Italy. In 1787 Goethe, traveling near Naples, lists the furniture which he saw in the living room of a small house at which he called as ". . . nicely woven cane chairs and, besides, a chest, gilded all over and painted with brightly colored flowers and then varnished". Flower designs seem to have been the most commonly employed.

Although the major states in Italy tended to develop their own styles in furniture the demands of similar social groups, in particular the very wealthy, were sometimes met in similar ways. Sofas of great length were produced in both Venice and Sicily to stand along ballroom walls. Those of Venice often incorporated multiple chair-backs joined together by a serpentine top rail, whereas the Sicilian variety employed an overall sculptural design. Gilding was normal for these pieces in both states but Venice also produced fine examples in plain carved wood.

Sicily has one of the most complicated cultural histories in Europe. By the 18th century the country had been dominated by Greeks, Carthaginians, Romans, Goths, Byzantines, Moors, Normans, Germans, by the French and by the Spaniards. In 1714 the Duke of

A cabinet-cum-drawing table made by Piffetti c1732 for the Queen's Closet in the Palazzo Reale in Turin, Piedmont. It reveals Piffetti's obsession for covering every surface with decoration; there are Rococo motifs of curling leaves and sphinxes with wings, and the wood is both painted and gilded. The tables have gilt bronze feet and the mounts are of gilt bronze too. The impression of complexity is increased by the mirrors on the walls and pillars reflecting the design.

Savoy became King of Sicily and brought to his capital, Turin, the last great Sicilian architect, Juvara, in whose work the eclectically based magnificence of Sicilian style gained homogeneity from the influence of his teacher of architectural design, Guarini. In Turin and its surrounding district Juvara designed churches and palaces, and, for the latter, a collection of furniture, in particular for two Piedmontese palaces; the Royal Palace in Turin and Stupinigi. The leading cabinet-maker for the House of Savoy for much of the century was Carlo Piffetti, who worked for the Kings of Sardinia (as the Dukes became in 1720 when they surrendered Sicily to the Austrians) from 1731 to his death in 1777. Piffetti's work combines the vitality of Sicilian and

NEOCLASSICAL

Southern Italian styling; his habit of decorating every available surface with an almost French delicacy of execution reveals that he may also have been influenced by the French tastes of Piedmontese/Savoyard society.

A second cabinet-maker who carried out superb work for the House of Savoy was Giuseppe Maria Bonzanigo, who was working in Turin by 1773 and became official woodworker to the Crown in 1787. His earlier work is in a style half way between Rococo and Louis XVI Neoclassicism. He exercised a conscious virtuosity and his craftsmanship was meticulous. His finest pieces are delicately carved and painted and

A firescreen by Bonzanigo. Made for the Palazzo Reale in Turin in c1775, it is of carved and gilt walnut. Bonzanigo was one of the few cabinet-makers whose work equaled that of the French, the Germans and the English, though his details are busier than theirs. Garlands of flowers often appear on Italian Rococo furniture, but the diapering effect was particular to Bonzanigo.

A fine quality Neoclassical marquetry chest-of-drawers of the style associated with the name of Maggiolini. His pieces are severely rectangular, beautifully veneered, and of excellent craftsmanship.

often incorporate a diamond checker inlay of various woods. He continued working through the French conquest and occupation and the subsequent restoration of the House of Savoy in 1814.

The 18th-century excavations at Pompeii and Herculaneum lent impetus to the revival of the use of Classical motifs in what was considered to be a "correct" Antique style. In England Robert Adam introduced an elegant and restrained version of Neoclassicism, which was to be influential through much of the continent. In Italy, however, Neoclassicism was nearer to the Roman work of the Imperial Age than to the Graeco-Roman (or "Etruscan" as it was often erroneously called) inspiration of Adam and his imitators. Italy was encouraged to follow Imperial patterns by the publication, in 1769, of Piranesi's drawings of the decorations on Roman buildings, where the elaborate mixture of motifs current under the Roman Empire was resurrected.

ITALY AND SPAIN

Despite the influence of Piranesi, grandeur without fussiness was the tone of some of the most magnificent furniture of the late 18th century. The bronze table made in 1789–90 by Valadier and Pacetti for the Pope is probably the most famous example.

From the mid century scagliola (marble paste) had been developed in Florence to provide a cheaper substitute for *pietre dure*, particularly for table tops. It was a flexible enough medium to allow work to be undertaken which combined much of the delicacy of painting with the hardness of marble. It proved immensely popular with the tourist trade, those English and other European patrons, wealthy enough to enjoy the Grand Tour and buy such furniture as pleased them.

Florentine furniture in general stands apart from the whole-hearted Baroque and Rococo work of the rest of Italy. Its early 18th-century seat furniture was often angular rather than rounded. Later in the century, under the influence of the English pattern books of Chippendale, Hepplewhite and Sheraton, Florentine furniture approximated more closely to the work of other Italian cities.

During the 1760s in Milan the best-known Italian marquetry designer of the second half of the century, Giuseppe Maggiolini, began designing furniture in which a restrained Classicism was delicately applied to case furniture. His pieces are usually severely rectangular, the veneers chosen with great care and the standard of craftsmanship bears comparison with that of contemporary English and French work.

Spain and Portugal

Spanish, and to a lesser degree, Portuguese furniture has been influenced by the long dominance of the Moors in Spain. Portugal expelled them in 1249, Spain only in 1492. They left a legacy of fine leather work and a love of intricate abstract curvilinear patterns. Whereas this common element in the political past of the two countries left a common legacy, diverging political interests led to different tastes in furniture. Spain's empire was built in Europe first, and Italian influence is clear on her furniture. When Spanish conquests extended to Mexico and Peru, gold and silver flooded in but the influence of the aboriginal inhabitants was minimal. Portugal turned to the East and formed a trading empire with the ancient civilizations of India, China and the Spice Islands. Besides becoming wealthy, a

Classical amorini supported cartouches in which noble families, from the popes downwards, applied their coats of arms.

Mythological monsters, harpies, nymphs, gods, chimeras and sphinxes decorated walls and furnishings.

The ancient lion's paw foot now the usual base for Italian chests.

RENAISSANCE ITALY AND SPAIN

Classical columns and pediments were applied to architecturally conceived cabinets.

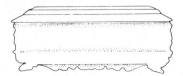

In Italy the Classical sarcophagus shape became a clothes chest.

Spain over-used applied sculpture. Gothic and Classical forms were mixed together.

Motifs and shapes were taken directly from Classical architecture to decorate contemporary furniture. Columns were derived from the Classical orders. Forms of ancient sarcophagi were adapted for clothes chests. Mythology was ransacked for fabulous beasts to carve and paint. Painters often decorated furniture. In both countries chestnut and oak were used. There was much gilding of furniture in Italy. In Spain the Classical past combined with the Moorish legacy to form a hybrid style, intricate, sometimes hysterically obsessive in its application of decorative motifs.

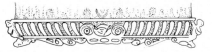

Gadrooning—a Classical pattern—decorated the base and under-lid of cassone.

The Moorish, mudejar style of inlay was still used in Spain.

Another Spanish hybrid; the boxwood medallion—called Romayne work in England—used in a mudejar style cabinet.

PORTUGAL

love of the exotic developed and there was a great influx of lacquer and oriental porcelain into the country. In the 18th century Portugal developed a second empire in Brazil which provided wealth in the form of diamonds and brought in the almost black hardwood adopted by furniture makers for some of their intricate turned work.

The union of the two countries from 1580 to 1640 gave them some experiences in common but in furniture their differences remained greater than their similarities. Portugal's trade with England, the English factories at Lisbon and Oporto and Catherine of Braganza's return to Portugal with her English furniture after the death of her husband, Charles II of England, created a deep English influence on Portuguese furniture whether for the court, the upper or the middle classes. In Spain the end of the Spanish royal house in 1700 and the accession of the House of Bourbon brought French influence into furniture making for the court but had little effect elsewhere.

A Spanish cabinet of the first half of the 16th century. The decoration of the outer wings is called plateresque, the term describing an inlay of delicate curvilinear abstract pattern. The roundels were known as Romayne work.

A 17th-century fruitwood table. The form of bracing, decorative sprung-iron brackets, was a common feature. In this case the decoration, which is of leaves and tendrils, is fairly elaborate. Many pieces were much simpler in design. The shape of the legs with their carved ends is also typical, though once again this example is quite ornate.

It is impossible to say much about Portuguese furniture before the 17th century since wars and earthquakes have destroyed too much. It is known that strong oriental influences were at work from Portugal's past and from her overseas Empire and that ivory inlays in the *mudejar* style—a non-representational style of intricate geometric patterns—were applied to chairs and cupboards in both Spain and Portugal. A further Moorish inheritance shared by both countries was the use of *guadamecil* (tooled and stamped) leather for chairs and chests. Spanish and Portuguese craftsmen—Spanish in particular—were skilled in the use of curvilinear "plateresque" inlays: these were delicate curvilinear abstract geometric or flower-like geometric inlays. Portugal produced decoration of what in England at the same period was called "Romayne Work", portrait profiles carved in roundels, probably taken from Italy either directly or via France.

Some 16th-century Spanish furniture is extant and exemplifies the common factor of contemporary work throughout Western Europe: the application of Renaissance motifs taken from Italy to essentially Medieval pieces of furniture. However, two original forms of cabinet were developed: the *vargueño* and the *papeleira*. Each consisted of a rectangular box containing a series of drawers and, often, one or more small cupboards. The *vargueño* had a drop front, which the *papeleira* lacked. Both types were usually placed on a stand and often decorated with *mudejar* marquetry. In the 17th century the *papeleira* approximated more and more to the Antwerp cabinet. Ebony veneers and tortoiseshell-fronted drawers .became common, al-

though a specifically Iberian form of decoration of pierced brass mounts, usually surrounding a handle, was sometimes added to each drawer front. The Portuguese were particularly fond of this form of decoration. They also liked turned decoration; cabinet stands, table legs and above all bedposts and rails were all produced with elaborate turned designs. In Portugal the dominance of fabrics in providing splendor to beds was superseded by the paramountcy of fine turned wood.

It is thought that 16th-century Spanish and Portuguese tables were of the simple trestle type, although some columnar-legged tables of the refectory kind survive. Even in grand interiors of the mid-17th century trestle tables seem to have been usual with decoration provided by an oriental rug spread over them if the owner could afford it. The Velazquez full-length portrait of Philip IV in the London National Gallery illustrates this fashion.

In the 17th century Spain produced a variant on the trestle table in which the trestles were joined to the top and to each other by a decorative wrought iron stretcher or strut. The folding X-frame chair (*sillón de cadera*) was introduced from Italy early in the 16th century but the best known chair made in Spain at the same period was the *sillón de fraileros*. This was a square or rectangular framed armchair (towards the end of the century an armless variety also appeared) with

Right: Spanish chairs. *Top*: A *sillón de cadera*, a Spanish X frame chair of the early 16th century. It is hung with fringed brocade and the decoration of the frame is in *mudejar* inlay.

Bottom right: A mid-18th-century Spanish adaptation of an English design. Some of the decorative detail is gilded, which distinguishes it from its English prototype.

Bottom left: A chair by Gasparini, one of a set from the royal palace in Madrid. The legs show the influence of the Louis XV *fauteuil*.

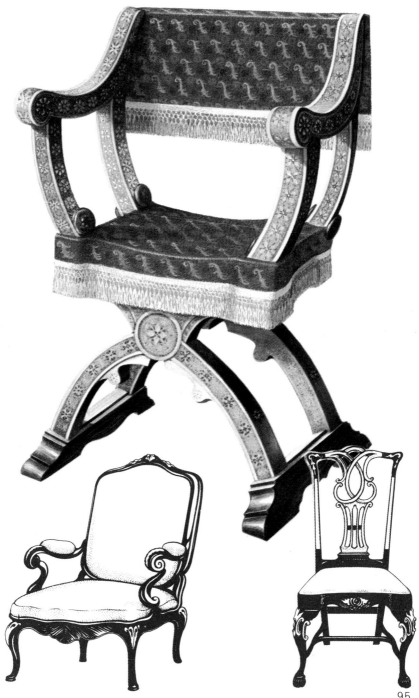

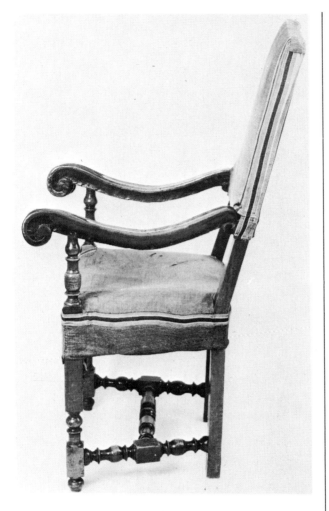

A Spanish 17th-century chair, a development of the monks' chair, the *sillón de fraileros*. The shape of the arms with a large volute at each hand is Baroque. The bobbin turning of the stretchers was a common form of turned work in Spain in the 17th century.

the back and seat covered in fringed fabric, often of velvet or leather. Decoratively headed nails were used to attach the covering. Stretchers between the legs and the rails emphasized the rectangularity of the construction. This type of chair continued to be made through the 17th century. An example can be seen in Velazquez's portrait of the Infant Philip Prosper in Vienna.

The Portuguese love of turned work is evident in 17th-century chairs. In Portuguese hands the *sillón de fraileros* gained turned legs and stretchers and sometimes ball feet. Its back became slimmer, taller and more elegant, with an arched top and brass decorations. Having taken a Spanish design and transformed it the Portuguese then proceeded to influence Spanish design with their transformed version.

English influence, particularly in the design of seat furniture, was felt in most parts of Europe in the second half of the 18th century. In Portugal English influence began considerably earlier. English lacquer furniture was being exported to Spain and Portugal before the end of the 17th century and there was a considerable trade in non-oriental-inspired English furniture even earlier. The Portuguese followed English patterns but at a distance, taking inspiration from them rather than directly copying them. Thus a distinctively Portuguese version of Queen Anne chairs evolved using Brazilian hardwoods. At first these were very close to the originals, but they rapidly adopted more exaggerated curves for cabriole legs, which were made of thinner wood, and surmounted the English splat back with a sculptured flourish. Later in the century Chippendale patterns were adopted and provided with extravagant sculptured detail or even with painted and gilded ornament. By the end of the century painted Neoclassical seat furniture in the style of Hepplewhite became fashionable. An English idea for dual use furniture, the sofa which unfolds to make a bed, seems to have been greatly to Portuguese taste from the number of surviving examples. Portuguese beds, however, continued to defy any foreign influence and developed into something which, in retrospect, looks remarkably like a Victorian bed without posts, and with a sculpted and sometimes partly padded headboard as the dominant feature.

By the middle of the 18th century French influence is apparent in some Portuguese armchairs and in the indiscriminate application of Rococo ornament—even to chairs which are Queen Anne in style. French influence on the furniture of the Spanish court was more profound. Louis XV armchairs were particularly popular. On storage furniture French influence was supplemented by Italian richness and weight. Gasparini's work for the Royal Palace in Madrid from 1768 drew on French prototypes and his sofas and chairs conform closely to their originals. His commodes, however, display the strong curves and exuberant marquetry of Southern Italy. Spanish Neoclassical furniture is also nearer to that of Southern Italy than to that of France.

These chairs are examples of Portuguese work.

Top: A mid-18th-century French influenced Portuguese armchair with one slightly unusual feature—the piercing of the back which was influenced by English Gothicism. In the 18th century the forms of Portuguese chairs were influenced by both France and England.

Left; A late 17th-century chair. The back and seat are of embossed leather, the front legs have ball feet and the stretchers have bobbin turning. These are all conventional Portuguese forms, as is the complicated carving of the front stretcher.

Right: A mid-18th-century chair strongly influenced by English fashion, but with the design given a distinctive Portuguese flavor by the cresting on the rail and the carvings around the bottom of the apron.

The Low Countries

In the 15th century the major towns of the Low Countries were firmly independent. Their statutes gave their councils considerable power and within the town a culture of the "haute bourgeoisie" came into being. Yet the whole area was part, and the richest part, of the lands of the Duke of Burgundy. Partly financed by the richest of the towns the dukes of the period developed the most splendid court culture in Europe. There was a rift between these two cultures, widened by the Reformation. The dukes remained Catholic, as did the Southern cities; the Northern cities became predominantly Protestant. When at the end of the century Burgundy became first Austrian and then Spanish, the Low Countries revolted.

The 16th century was torn by religious and political upheavals until in 1579 the predominantly Protestant North became virtually independent and in 1609 became a republic. The South remained Catholic and closely associated with Spain.

Despite civil strife the 16th century saw great developments in the arts. By 1580 Hans Vredeman de Vries had produced designs which revolutionized furniture styles in the Low Countries and affected those of France and England. The Low Countries had been the center of an exuberant gothicism. De Vries applied Classical ornament to furniture. He was an architect and ornamentalist. Carved chimeras, nudes, Classical masks and garlands and classically derived canopies decorate his beds. Sculpted niches, into which a Classical architect might have inserted statuary, are carved in a bed head. He applied wide bulbs to furniture legs, a preference which was enormously influential in England, Scandinavia and Germany, much used on tables and chairs; he also virtually created strapwork, a geometric interlacing of curves and straight lines usually carved in low relief. This spread equally widely. His son, Paul Vredeman de Vries, continued the forms created by his father in the furniture designs which he published in 1630.

In the 17th century the independent-mindedness of the cities became evident in their applied arts. The guilds were strong and in each city the guild members seem to have had a measure of agreement on how they saw their own forms of furniture developing. Probably the most well-known type of furniture to be produced in the 17th century and certainly the most spectacular,

A Dutch 17th-century Antwerp cabinet. The inlay is of tortoiseshell and wood. There are gilt bronze keyhole surrounds and gilt bronze terms on the front. The eight-legged base, contemporary with the cabinet, has flattened bun feet and is ebony inlaid with tortoiseshell and different woods. Eight legs were often used for 17th-century stands, as were square section baluster legs.

was the Antwerp cabinet. These were produced in large numbers and were exported to most countries in Western Europe. They consisted of a cabinet formed of a series of small drawers arranged in a grid pattern, often with one or two small cupboards in the center, placed on a stand. They were usually veneered in ebony with the drawer fronts veneered in tortoiseshell, often backed with foil for greater brilliance. Semiprecious stones and ivory could also be used. Sometimes the whole or the major part of the front was enclosed by doors. Sometimes the drawer fronts and the insides of doors were painted. Although Antwerp was the major center for production of these cabinets they were made elsewhere. However, the city was the great distribution point for them to the world at large. In the early part of the century Antwerp also produced low buffets heavily carved with stylized fruit and flowers within an overall architectural form and cupboards in two stages which consist of two sets of cupboards ranged one above the other, the doors decorated with intarsia panels.

The province of Holland (then only one of the provinces forming the country which now bears its name) produced the *Beeldenkast*, a cupboard divided into an upper and a lower stage, decorated with carved scenes of human life and with caryatids. These cupboards were the work of the cabinet-maker and the carver, a differentiation on which the guild rules were strict; each man had his appropriate work. Often the cupboards have flattened bun feet. They are luxury objects but on the whole the decoration of pieces from the Northern provinces (modern Holland) are more restrained than those from the South, although in the 17th century the rise of the House of Orange there provided a court to encourage the production of luxuries. It was in the South that connections with Spain and Italy were maintained, although some Spanish and Moorish influence is apparent in the geometric moldings characteristically used on chests in the Northern province of Zeeland.

A cabinet-on-stand, c1690, by the Dutch cabinet-maker Jan van Mekeren. It is a very fine example of Dutch floral marquetry, a subject popular in contemporary painting too. The wrinkled ribbon motif in the center was often employed, though this is a particularly detailed example. The stand is partly veneered in ebony, as is the background to the two large panels.

BAROQUE

In the second half of the 17th century in the Northern provinces the *Beeldenkast* declined in use as cupboards resembling 19th- or early 20th-century wardrobes came into use. These had two tall doors forming the major part of the front. The carcase was usually of oak. Luxury examples were often wholly or partly veneered in ebony. Tall cabinets on stands which became fashionable towards the end of the 17th century introduce a new element in the use of wood in Dutch furniture; the material was cut to display its figure to best advantage and delicate geometric marquetries of exotic woods were used to veneer the whole surface of a piece of furniture.

In the 17th century the impact of the Baroque on furniture was enormous. Tables, chairs and beds underwent a transformation. The best known surviving tables of the first half of the century are solid affairs, usually made in oak, with the bulbous legs associated with the work of Vredeman de Vries. In contrast, by the 1670s in the Northern provinces, where the "auricular" style was popular, side tables were produced with this decoration on the supports. The style gains its name from the oddly boneless curves and whorls of which it is made, like the curves of the ear. These swags and scoops often carry carved vegetation or sections of birds and feathers and the whole constitutes a rather fleshy amalgam.

By the 1680s the full Baroque is displayed in superbly gilded tables; beautifully carved caryatids or putti and great swags of flowers hold up tops of exquisitely etched brass and tortoiseshell marquetry. This was introduced to Holland by the Huguenot refugees from France after the Revocation of the Edict of Nantes in 1685.

At the beginning of the 17th century three basic chair types existed; the armless rectangular chair with a leather or upholstered seat and a back panel that was sometimes leather covered; the rectangular armchair with upholstered seat and back; and the X-chair, whose ancestry derived from the Italian Renaissance version of the Roman curule chair. This was sometimes fixed but sometimes folded. Walnut, ebony or rosewood were used in the construction of these chairs and they almost invariably have lion finials on the back. The legs of rectangular chairs are usually made up of vase-shaped sections.

By the end of the 17th century the basic chair shape

Three Dutch chairs. *Left*: An early 18th-century Dutch elm armchair with upholstery on the seat and armrests. The pierced back splat shows English influence, but the cabriole leg ending in a hoof is a Dutch invention. The outward turning angle of the arms is greater than in the equivalent English chair, and the curves of the back and seat are more complex.

Top right: A Spanish-inspired Netherlandish chair of the early 17th century. Usually made in walnut, some, like this one, are of ebony. It has double baluster legs and is a square-framed chair, resembling a *sillón de fraileros*. The back and seat are of tooled leather, stretched and nailed into position.

Bottom right: A Dutch armchair c1780 in the Louis XVI style, made of mahogany. The fluted legs are particularly French in style. The little rectangular apron does not altogether fit with its carved decorative wreath.

Left: An early 17th-century carved oak Dutch armchair. Sea motifs, common in Baroque work, here run riot. The legs are an unusual shape, ending in the form of a fish: the arms are in the shape of dolphins. At the back are turned balusters.

Right: A cane-backed Dutch chair of the late 17th century. The influence of Daniel Marot, the designer and architect, is apparent in the tall thin back, the wide seat and the use of the Baroque shell motif at the top. Velvet upholstery and fringing were often used.

Far right: An Anglo-Dutch walnut chair, c1725. The upholstery is secured with decorative brass nail heads. A shell motif is carved on the knee. Pierced decorative splats were also popular.

was a low upholstered seat on legs of varying section joined by curved and carved stretchers and a tall, thin undulating back, heavily carved with shells and acanthus leaves sometimes overall and sometimes as a surround to a cane panel. These tall-backed chairs are often associated with the name of Daniel Marot, a Huguenot refugee to the court of William of Orange, who accompanied William to England on his accession to the English throne. Marot's work covers a spectacularly wide array of the decorative arts. In furniture he used drapery to great effect. For four-poster beds he replaced intricately carved wood with great pelmets of Genoa velvet crowned with ostrich plumes and used magnificent hangings and coverlets.

In the late 17th and early 18th centuries the political and social interactions between Holland and England encouraged a cross-fertilization of ideas which makes it difficult to assign a definite origin to many particular

pieces. In the main, Dutch chairs have more pronounced curves in the back splat and in the sides
than English work, and Dutch bureaux-book-
cases, unlike their English prototype, were regularly
veneered with a complex parquetry of exotic woods.

The main developments of the general appearance of
Dutch furniture during the 18th century follow the
French example. The Baroque, which continued into
the early part of the century, was superseded in mid
century by the more delicate decorative motifs of the
Rococo. But Dutch cabinet work in general was more
bombé (convex) than similar French work and English
influence continued to be exerted, to be seen in the use
of the claw and ball foot on cabriole legs and in the
development of specialized tea-tables. By 1780. as in
France and England the outline of chests-of-drawers,

An 18th-century Dutch *bombé* chest-of-drawers. The Dutch were particularly fond of the *bombé* shape and this is a restrained example of a taste that could reach dropsical proportions. The high quality mounts are of gilt bronze. Those on the front feet are for decoration and to protect the corners where veneers are particularly vulnerable.

tables and chairs became straighter and plain mahogany grew in popularity during the Classical revival. The Dutch also followed the prevailing fashion for incorporating lacquer panels in case and table furniture. Since for two centuries they had been the major importers to Europe of fine oriental wares it is surprising that they had not used them earlier to the same extent as the English and the French.

In 1771 the Dutch declared the import of furniture illegal. The guilds had been complaining for some time of the competition from English and French cabinet-makers. This law however, did not prevent the Dutch from keeping pace with stylistic developments abroad; the range of furniture types was expanded in Holland at the same time as in England and France. The fall-front secretary and the tea-table are two pieces which were introduced and immediately became popular.

From the Austrian Netherlands (the Southern provinces) fewer examples of fine furniture remain. One distinctive piece produced in the South in the mid-18th century was the massive double-doored wardrobe, finely covered with an all-over veneer and delicately carved in the French Rococo manner.

The most distinctive feature of Netherlands furniture as a whole in the 18th century was the use of fine veneers. Parquetry patterns never became completely unfashionable even when burr wood or mahogany were the most desirable materials in the eyes of the *haute bourgeoisie*. Some of the distinctiveness of Dutch furniture disappeared when Neoclassicism was introduced, but with this movement national variations throughout Europe began to be eroded.

Germany
Until the unification of Germany in the 19th century, the country was divided into a multitude of states whose rulers owed allegiance, in varying degrees, to the Hapsburg Emperor in Vienna. This system prevailed until the Holy Roman Empire was destroyed by Napoleon. Some states were ecclesiastical, ruled over by Prince Bishops whose major allegiance was to the Pope; some Imperial towns were controlled by groups of burgesses; other states were ruled directly by the Emperor as Hapsburg lands or by enormously powerful princely families, such as the Wittelsbachs and Hohenzollerns. Not surprisingly, local schools of work developed in many of the major states and cities. The Reformation, during which each state took up a Catholic or Protestant identity, made little difference to the furniture produced for the aristocracy and the better-off middle classes. It is unlikely that much furniture was owned by people below that standing.

A factor common to all German furniture in the first half of the 16th century was the use of Renaissance ornament. The woodcuts produced c1530 by the designer known as Master H.S. show plans for cupboards and beds in which Gothic pinnacles and tracery have disappeared. Columns that are Classical in appearance flank severely geometrical cupboard doors. In Nuremberg Peter Flötner produced ornamental designs in which Renaissance putti disport themselves amongst stylized tendrils and foliage, designs probably inspired by contemporary Italian manuscript illumination. A comparison between inspiration and result is revealing. Where the Italian original expresses an open acceptance of the physical world, the elaboration of the German copy suggests something akin to hysteria. A compulsive emphasis on detail in preference to overall

design is a common feature of much German furniture of the 16th century. It is particularly true of the technically superb perspective intarsia work of Augsburg and Nuremberg which was applied to chests and cabinets.

The productions of the German states can be roughly divided into two major groups. Northern Germany used predominantly hardwoods, particularly oak, or for some carved work, walnut. The furniture is strongly constructed and depends for decoration on work carved out of the solid wood. In Southern Germany softwoods were more widespread and to give protection against worm and damp furniture was often either painted or overlaid with a marquetry of harder woods.

In the early 16th century benches seem to have been the usual form of seating, but since furniture was sparse they were put to a number of uses. In Dürer's woodcut of the *Birth of the Virgin* a chest is used, not only, presumably, as a container, but also as a seat on which a woman is reclining and as a back to a low bench on which another woman is sitting. The construction of the chest is indicated by the clearly shown dovetail joints.

Later in the century benches were replaced by chairs. Later still, heavily carved fruitwood chairs adapted from Italy seem to have been fashionable. Their hard wooden seats and little sloping backs suggest that they were made for display rather than comfort.

Above: A table composed of two parts. The table itself was made in Augsburg in 1626 and is of ebony and other woods. The top, of *pietre dure*, was made in Prague in 1580. Amongst the different semi-precious stones are lapis-lazuli, jasper and agate.

Right: A panel from the Wrangelschrank cabinet, made in Augsburg in 1566. The city specialized in perspective intarsia work. Many different woods were used on this panel, some stained green or shaded by burning.

Most beds throughout Germany in the 16th century were of either the built-in or the box type. The bedroom served as the principal reception room in the private house with the heavily carved bed as its main feature. Sometimes the bed was built into an angle of the room so that two of its sides were formed by the wainscotting of the walls. A few freestanding beds were made.

A speciality of Augsburg and Prague was the use of precious stones and metals for tables and cabinets. Frames were of wood. On the cabinets, panels of *pietre dure* or engraved rock crystal were flanked by rock crystal columns set in gold and gems. Table tops were formed of complex mosaics of semi-precious stones. Naturally such work was very expensive and highly prized. The Wrangelschrank cabinet, taken as booty in the Thirty Years War by the Swedish commander, Count Wrangel, is an extraordinary example of Augsburg work. Double columns flank carved boxwood panels. The whole of the front is enclosed by doors the inside of which consist of delicately executed "surrealist" intarsia extravaganzas.

Northern Germany, throughout the first half of the 17th century, continued to produce tall, heavily carved cupboards. Massive in size, like the Dutch *Beeldenkast* cabinets they carry standing figures as part of their decoration.

The Thirty Years' War of 1618–48 spread chaos through the states. At its end a new social division had

A mid-17th-century cabinet from Eger in Bohemia. The city was famous for a specific form of sculptured inlay. Two or more different kinds of wood were employed to form a colóred picture in relief. The scenes on this cabinet, which would have been placed on a stand, depict the months of the year. The central scene is of Adam and Eve after the Fall. Each panel forms a drawer front; in the center is a cupboard.

A cembalo case made by Gerhard Dagly, c1700. Dagly specialized in producing a white lacquer with oriental scenes painted on in color, as in this example. The result was nothing like oriental lacquer, but instead resembled porcelain. Dagly's best work was produced for the King of Prussia.

come into being. In most of Germany, particularly in the South and East, the princely houses now dominated the towns. In the North, the great towns had maintained and strengthened their middle-class culture. But even within the princely areas some towns maintained their own tradition of working. At Eger, situated where the royal areas of Bohemia, the Palatinate and Saxony meet, cabinets were decorated with highly individual intarsia panels, the work being carved in relief instead of only existing in two dimensions.

The states nearest to the Netherlands produced furniture reflecting the decorative forms of their neighbors. The great fruitwood cupboards of the Trèves area in the late 17th century with their double wardrobe-like doors are similar to Dutch work except for two small drawers set side by side below the main cupboard.

Applied or carved decoration in a restrained version of the Netherlandish auricular style is often found on them. Dutch influence was also apparent in work commissioned in the mid-17th century by the Elector Frederick William of Prussia for his palace in Berlin. The most elegant of Berlin furniture, however, was of Far Eastern influence. In 1687 Gerard Dagly began to make lacquer furniture for Frederick of Prussia. Dagly's work was technically far superior to most of the japanning carried out in Europe. Although he borrowed figures and motifs from oriental work the results are far from being mere imitations of misunderstood originals. Some of his loveliest work is executed on a white ground in imitation of porcelain, and incorporates japanned colored figures.

The *Millionenzimmer* in Schonbrunn Palace in Vienna, an example of the very grandest of 18th-century Rococo decoration. Made for the Empress Maria Theresa, the paneling is formed of exotic woods. The "cut outs" in the wood each contain a framed Indian miniature. This paneling is said to have cost a million

thalers, from which the room derives its name. The furniture is Austrian, c1740. The shapes of the chairs show strong French influence—the two armchairs were called *fauteuils à la reine* in France—but the over-elaboration of Rococo detail is Austrian, as is the overall gilding of the table.

In the second half of the 17th century Bavaria had close connections with Savoy and Piedmont. From fine Italian Baroque furniture the use of human figures as supports for tables was adopted, as was a sculptural style. Italian influence also encouraged the Southern German love of fine marble mosaic for table tops. However, by the end of the century the Bavarian court was more susceptible to Parisian influence. In the early years of the 18th century the Elector acquired Boulle furniture, while marquetries of brass and tortoiseshell were being produced in Munich in imitation of the work of Bérain and Boulle.

Responsibility for the emulation of Parisian style rests primarily with the architects and designers Joseph Effner and François Cuvilliés the Elder. Effner was trained in Paris and his work reflects a love of contemporary French furnishings. Cuvilliés was perhaps the more important of the two. A Walloon, he was introduced to the court of Bavaria as court dwarf. The Elector recognized his abilities as a designer and sent him to study in Paris from 1720 to 1724. On his return he redesigned the interior and furnishings of the Residenz, the Elector's palace in Munich, and created the Amalienburg, a palace in the gardens of the Nymphenburg palace. His furniture was painted, gilded and carved. In his commodes, which recall the best Louis XV furniture, he achieved subtle outlines and a brilliant lightness of color, producing perhaps the finest German Rococo works. Where Effner's work recalls the furniture of the French Regency period, Cuvilliés' has all the rather feminine grace of the age of Mme de Pompadour.

From the 1740s to the 1760s the palaces of Berlin were decorated in a style usually known as "Frederican Rococo". Frederick II of Prussia was fortunate enough to acquire the services of a series of superb furniture designers and craftsmen. For five years, in the early 1740s, Johann August Nahl designed furniture and interiors at Potsdam. His work contains an element of fantasy. Palm fronds and winged dragons flicker in his wall decorations and the carved and pierced chairs made under his influence can be bizarre: the seats too deep, the legs too wavy; but they are undeniably exuberant.

In the 1750s Johann Michael and his brother Johann Christian Hoppenhaupt introduced fine, plain veneers, used both in their own right and as a foil for marquetry and gilt bronze. During the 1750s and early 1760s Johann Melchior Kambli produced magnificent ormolu. He used tortoiseshell veneers to set off a great display of delicately chased and gilded bronze mounts in the shape of trellises, festoons of flowers and curling acanthus leaves. Kambli also supplied mounts for the furniture of two great cabinet-makers who specialized in fine marquetry, the brothers Johann Friedrich and Heinrich Wilhelm Spindler. In their work marquetry and mounts are used to complement each other. The result can sometimes be too much of a feast for eyes accustomed to plain surfaces. Their surfaces are always busy. The quality of their craftsmanship, however, is always excellent.

Before moving to Berlin the Spindlers had worked in Bayreuth for the sister of Frederick the Great and her husband. Money was in shorter supply in Bayreuth than in Berlin and, whereas gilt bronze and fine marquetries were available to the Spindlers under their later employer, in Bayreuth they often worked in softwoods stained to imitate walnut and gilded to imitate ormolu.

Bayreuth stands at the east end of the long central strip of Germany in which "Franconian Rococo" was produced. Mainz was the Western tip and Bamberg, Würzburg and Ansbach formed the heart-land of the style. Here North Italian Baroque and French Rococo married to produce a vigorous, delicate, supremely lively style which is more sculptural than French Rococo and displays craftsmanship superior to that of almost any furniture produced in 18th-century Italy. The great central example of Franconian Rococo is the decoration and furnishing of the great Baroque palace of the Prince Bishops at Würzburg. Here furniture to complement the architecture of Johann Lucas van Hildebrandt and the ceilings painted by Tiepolo was produced by Wolfgang van der Auvera, Carl Maximilian Mattern and Johann Georg Nestfell.

The social and political center of the German world and of the Austro-Hungarian Empire was Vienna. As capital of a multi-national empire Vienna looked to France as the center of international style for the first three-quarters of the 18th century, after which English influence became more pronounced. As the domestic center of Austria the city developed a middle-class furniture style. To some extent this copied English fashions, particularly after the publication in 1787 of the Weimar-based *Journal des Luxus und der Moden*,

David Roentgen's upright secretaire, which dates from the second half of the 1770s. There are strong Rococo influences in the asymmetrical marquetries, and in the naturalistic representation of flowers and leaves. But the rectangular shape of the piece is Neoclassical; so too are the motifs of the gilt bronze mounts, strings of husks at the top, acanthus leaves above the feet, and tiny rosettes on the corners of the lower cupboards.

which extolled English fashion. Soon the style became specifically and elegantly Viennese. Much court furniture made before the 1780s is difficult to ascribe to France or Austria. From that time the Neoclassical elegance of English furniture, which had already influenced non-court furniture in Vienna, was adopted to produce pieces in which the straight line replaced Rococo curves, Wedgwood jasperware medallions were incorporated into items of furniture and the careful balancing of rectangular elements was regarded as more important than displays of virtuosity.

In the 18th century the first great international furniture firm was created in Germany. Abraham Roentgen was trained as a cabinet-maker in Holland and England. He opened his own workshop in Neuwied in 1750, where he was joined by his son David in 1761. This workshop may be seen as the prototype of today's

FRANCE

great multi-national companies. Furniture makers had often traveled abroad before and had worked in different countries. David Roentgen not only traveled widely, but in order to fulfill orders he set up workshops as subsidiaries of the Neuwied plant in St Petersburg, Brussels and Berlin. In Paris he was received into the guild of *ébénistes*. He also established warehouses for his goods in a number of the main towns in Germany so that local patrons could inspect his stock and make their choice. Primarily his patrons were the princes of Europe.

Both Abraham and David Roentgen's designs, particularly for writing desks, were well-known for their use of ingenious machinery to raise, lower or alter the functions of parts of the piece. David's early predilection was for superbly executed marquetry in the Rococo manner. In the late 1770s he began to favor Neoclassical designs. From the 1780s until his death in 1807 he employed more severe overall veneers of finely figured woods.

France

The spread of Renaissance ideas from Italy to France was initially the result of the response of the French King François I (1515–47). For some time the adoption of Renaissance ideas was confined to the court and its members. Provincial works and the art and furniture of people outside the circle of court and nobility were affected far more slowly.

François I deliberately set out to become a Renaissance prince with fashionable surroundings in the Italian manner. At Fontainebleau, his favorite palace, he employed Italian artists to provide him with such surroundings and Italian and Flemish influences dominated French court furniture until the early 17th century. Flemish influences were the result of trade and economic pressures. Besides the king three other strong personalities supported this policy: Marie de Medici, the Florentine wife of Henri IV, who became Regent on her husband's death in 1610; Anne of Austria, the wife of Louis XIII (1610–43) whose connections with the Low Countries were close and who also became Regent of France; and the great Cardinal Mazarin whose government lasted from 1643–61. All four favored rich materials and fine decoration and all four looked especially to Italy as the source of elegance. The two best known 16th-century French designers of furniture, du Cerceau and Sambin, re-

Pietre dure panels and gilt-bronze mounts were used for cabinets and prie-dieux.

Floral marquetry spread from the Low Countries through Baroque Europe.

Volutes, shells and garlands, common Baroque motifs, continued well into the 18th century.

The grand furniture of 17th-century Europe is probably the most magnificent ever made. Forms are curvaceous, decoration is exuberant. Sculpture was heavily used, both as applied decoration and as supports. Rich materials, pietre dure, *gold, silver, lacquer, fine marquetries, tortoiseshell and ivory were employed by superb craftsmen. Gilded wood was popular, so was silver furniture and upholstery of Genoa velvet.*

Precious marbles, painted and inserted in cabinets, made furniture into works of art.

The first commode was created by Boulle in the early 18th century. The sculptural extravagance of Baroque work was later simplified.

Stretchers, complex in form, were used on seat furniture throughout the 17th century.

The same motifs run through Baroque art, whether for legs of cabinet stands and chairs or for use in architecture.

sponded to the fashion for things Italian by producing in the one case designs strongly influenced by Classical architecture and in the other designs in which elongated and fantastic figures recall the paintings of the Italian Mannerists. There is no extant furniture made directly after the designs of either man but a few pieces exist which resemble their work. A cupboard in the Frick Collection in New York looks as though it was inspired by Sambin, particularly in the extraordinary long-necked half-figures which flank the sides.

In the 16th century walnut was preferred to oak for most types of furniture. Chests and cupboards were supported on arcaded bases and decorated with crisply carved reliefs. Panels of Romayne work were popular.

A 16th-century French cupboard after Du Cerceau. The sculptural and architectural qualities of Du Cerceau's work are apparent in this piece, though it does not in fact follow any of his own designs. It combines an extraordinary mixture of styles. Attempted Classical details, such as the center pediment, are offset by the Mannerist broken reversed sections of pediment above. The cups have oddly Tibetan looking tops, in place of Classical urns. The caryatids are Renaissance and grotesque harpies flank the lower section.

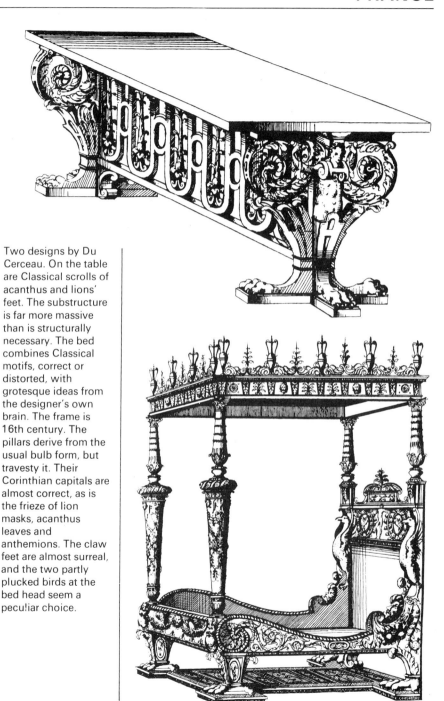

Two designs by Du Cerceau. On the table are Classical scrolls of acanthus and lions' feet. The substructure is far more massive than is structurally necessary. The bed combines Classical motifs, correct or distorted, with grotesque ideas from the designer's own brain. The frame is 16th century. The pillars derive from the usual bulb form, but travesty it. Their Corinthian capitals are almost correct, as is the frieze of lion masks, acanthus leaves and anthemions. The claw feet are almost surreal, and the two partly plucked birds at the bed head seem a peculiar choice.

119

LOUIS XIV

Chairs and tables became massive in size and then, in the second half of the century, armchairs became lighter. From paintings it can be seen that upholstered chairs were in use, though few survive. The *caquetoire*, a chair with a trapezoidal wooden seat, was developed to accommodate the enormous skirts of the period.

The main shapes of furniture changed little from the mid-16th century until a few years before the assumption of absolute power by Louis XIV in 1661. The Wars of Religion and the Fronde (the revolt of the nobility) paralyzed most creative activity at court although Marie de Medici, Anne of Austria, and Cardinal Mazarin influenced taste towards great opulence. Mazarin's collection of lacquer was outstanding.

In the 17th century lightly sculpted ebony became the usual veneer for luxury furniture. Hence the name *ébéniste* for "cabinet-maker". Precious metals and semi-precious stones encrusted the finest pieces. At the same time there was an increase in the use of turned decoration for table and chair legs, stretchers and decorative work. Moldings, which despite their name are a carved decoration, became heavier and in provincial work often covered the major part of a buffet or cabinet with a rather ungainly geometry. The pattern known as diamond point was particularly popular. Heavy cornices and flattened bun feet were typical of the period.

Chairs and armchairs began to be differentiated in contemporary references. Backs were usually low, except in the case of chairs of state, and fixed upholstery frequently took the place of hard seats and cushions. The *caquetoire* became known as the *chaise à vertugadin*. Its legs were turned and splayed and a garland of carved blooms became the normal back ornament. The first bureaux appeared, with flat tops and drawers set as a frieze or in a column below each end of the table.

Louis XIV 1643–1715 For the first twenty years of Louis XIV's reign Italian and Flemish influences on French furniture remained strong. Around 1660, however, the personalities and abilities of three men produced the necessary conditions for the development of an increasingly French style of furnishing.

Louis XIV denied political power to his aristocracy by keeping them constantly within arm's reach. The court became their cynosure and their home. An immense building program was begun which was to continue

One of a pair of cabinets made by Cucci c1681–83. The designs are of complete pictures with panels of birds, fruit, flowers and leaves and even two complete landscapes, all made of flat panels of *pietre dure*. The central compartment, a bowl of fruit, flowers and birds, is in relief. The royal cipher of two interlaced Ls surmounted by a crown is in gilt bronze; above it are trophies of war, also in gilt bronze.

through most of Louis' life. Furniture was needed in great quantities for his palaces; in order to reflect his political and social importance it had to be magnificent.

Colbert, Louis' chief minister from 1661, provided the economic foundation for realizing the king's requirements. In order to reduce France's import of luxury goods and to increase export potential in the same field he introduced a centralized and rigorous control over the quality of French manufactures. The most important agent of quality control was the *Manufacture Royale des Meubles de la Couronne*. Founded in 1667 this factory approved the design and execution of all furnishings made for the court. Its first director, the painter Charles le Brun, matched Louis' pretensions in the designs he made or authorized for suitable furnishings to frame the Sun King.

The central control of furniture production and the overall direction of King, Colbert and Le Brun, ensured a homogeneous style; the predominance of the designer over the craftsman and the artisan enabled interiors to be designed as a whole.

The furniture of the Italian-born *ébéniste* Domenico Cucci is even more sumptuous than that made in the reign of Louis XIII. However, a new sense of balance in form and color is achieved. The basic form employed for luxury storage furniture other than chests is still that of the Antwerp Cabinet but the simple grid pattern of equal sized drawer fronts of tortoiseshell set against an ebony background is replaced by a more sophisticated variation of drawer and cupboard sizes fronted with *pietre dure* and set off by a sumptuous pattern of ebony and gilt bronze.

In the first exuberant furnishing of the palace of Versailles quantities of furniture were made in solid silver. None remain there. In the course of Louis' European wars and the French Revolution it was all melted down for coin. However, a similar table was given to King Charles II of England and is now at Windsor Castle. The shapes employed are the same as were used for wooden furniture. Design in the 17th century was a matter of style to which materials were subordinated. Precious metals continued to be used for the surface decoration of furniture until the end of the 19th century. French decorative arts in the 17th century were called Classical rather than Baroque, but the scale of furnishings justifies use of the term Baroque. Most French Baroque furniture was squarely built.

A cupboard by Boulle in two tiers dated c1690. The quality of the piece is apparent in the superbly delicate veneer of ebony, pewter, engraved brass and blue-backed tortoiseshell. The interlaced Ls show that the piece was made for the royal household, if not for Louis XIV himself. The mask (top center) was a common motif; originally such mounts were intended to protect delicate edges of veneer—here it is purely decorative.

LOUIS XIV

One distinctive style of decoration which appeared at this time is associated with the name of André-Charles Boulle. He perfected a method of veneering furniture with a highly decorative combination of ebony, tortoiseshell, brass, pewter and mother-of-pearl, though not usually all on the same piece. Fine true veneers were produced. By glueing together sheets of the requisite materials and cutting them together, Boulle produced designs in which the sheets formed, alternately, the pattern and the ground, which resulted in a very delicate effect. Much of the furniture ascribed to Boulle is of a later date; only two fully documented pieces by him are known: a pair of commodes made in 1708–09 for the king's bedroom at Trianon, a separate small palace in the grounds of Versailles. Like Cucci, Boulle tended to give his furniture a strong central axis. However, he rejected the style of the Antwerp Cabinet. Instead of dividing each side of a cabinet into sections he created a new balance in the design by producing a near mirror image of some of the salient decorative features from one side on the other. The main outline of cabinet furniture remained square or rectangular: but the design was conceived of as a whole, with motifs carried from one side to the other.

The main pointers to quality in a piece of Boulle's work are: the exactness with which the veneers fit, the quality of the gilt bronze or brass mounts (if any); the contrasted use of high and low relief elements, and the ability to use a veneer to give the illusion of a further recessive plane. The cutting of the veneers should be smooth and even. Where there are large areas of tortoiseshell necessitating joining one piece to another without a covering section of brass, the joins should be so placed as to render them completely unobtrusive. Mounts should be crisply finished and it should be possible to follow the design through a series of recessive planes from the high relief sections (usually provided by the largest gilt bronze mounts) through mounts in a lower relief to the tortoiseshell ground whose figuring often gives a sense of depth. In some pieces a charming contrast is provided between a lively overall tendril-like inlay of brass or pewter and classically solemn gilt bronze mounts.

One very common feature of decoration at this time was introduced from the Low Countries by the furniture designer Jean Bérain, and adopted by Boulle and others. This is the use on large, flat surfaces of *singe-*

An example of Boulle's technique of veneering, with sheets forming, alternately, the pattern and the ground.

An early 18th-century cabinet, with doors probably by Boulle. The marquetry — including *singeries* — is in engraved brass, tortoiseshell and ebony. Such designs were not original to Boulle, being derived from the work of Jean Bérain. They always express very complex fantasies, and were enormously influential on Rococo designers. The top is of marble, which is unusual: such cabinets more often had ebony tops.

ries, patterns or scenes including figures of monkeys which are often depicted imitating the actions of human beings. These designs reflect the same taste for anthropomorphism as is shown by the popularity of La Fontaine's "Fables."

An important new material to appear in France at this time was lacquer. Cabinets imported at great expense from the Far East were broken up and their component parts set in furniture whose basic shapes remained steadfastly European. However, lacquer was not a major element in furniture design until the following reign.

As for cabinet furniture, the chest-of-drawers known as the commode was developed to become the most widely used container for household linen. Tall wardrobes or double cupboards (*armoires*) and the two kinds of bureaux continued to be made but now, at least in fashionable society, with Boulle decoration.

Seat furniture became slightly more specialized than under Louis XIII. Armchairs still looked like miniature thrones. They were massive, usually carved from wood,

Top: A Boulle-style *médailleur*, made for Louis XIV to store his medal collection. The gilt-bronze mounts at the top corners were to protect the veneer. The mask in the center is for decoration only.

Below: A detail of the *médailleur* to show the use of contrasts between high and low relief and the flat figured plane of tortoiseshell.

gessoed and gilded, with the seat and gently sloping high back covered with fabric. Stretchers were of an X or H shape and were sometimes extravagantly arched. Seats were wide and armrests heavily and often uncomfortably carved. A wide armchair or settee (*canapée*), able to accommodate two or three people, was developed.

Tables were made in many shapes and were lavishly decorated. Highly wrought legs, stretchers and aprons were the fashion and wood, marble and bronze were used as the basic materials for tables. These were now attached to walls as consoles and often had only two legs, meeting in the center in a graceful double curve. Table legs in general could be S shaped or made of caryatids or balusters. As with armchairs the weight of the superstructure, particularly in the case of marble-topped tables, made the provision of strong stretchers important. The X shape was the most common and on wooden furniture the cross-pieces were usually clamped to the legs, instead of being tenoned, for greater strength.

Regency and Louis XV 1715–1774   The death of the Sun King in 1715 and the regency of Phillippe, duc d'Orléans (1715–1723) herald in the greatest of all periods of furniture making.

Louis XIV's marriage to Madame de Maintenon in 1685 had established her gloomy reign at Versailles. Fashion ceased to be dominated by the court as courtiers escaped to the more entertaining life of the capital. For the last 30 years of Louis' life fashion became centered on Paris. The great nobles refurbished their Paris houses (the *noblesse de la robe* was Paris oriented already) and a new, rich middle class had grown up which demanded elegance and comfort. After the death of Louis XIV Phillippe d'Orléans encouraged the Parisward movement by setting up court in his own Paris house, the Palais Royal, and by transferring the five-year-old king to the Tuileries from Versailles. Louis XV moved the court back to Versailles and with the advent of Mme de Pompadour as royal mistress in 1745 Versailles was restored as the center of the arts and of fashion. This restoration was only successful because of the intelligence, taste and determination of the marquise.

One of the outstanding features of 18th-century France was the dominance of women in social life.

LOUIS XV

Whereas the 17th-century leaders of salons had been blue-stockings, their 18th-century equivalents were fashionable and political as well as intellectual. Entertaining became more domestic in style. The great *enfilades* of rooms opening one from another to form vistas were replaced by more intimate rooms. Private apartments furnished for comfort and elegance rather than for grandeur became the most important rooms in private houses for living in and receiving. To some extent this was true of palaces. The *petits appartements* at Versailles were created for the king and his most intimate friends, not for the whole gaggle of courtiers. Rooms of this kind led to the small scale of much Louis XV and XVI furniture and to the feminine influence the prettiness of much of it is due. This influence is particularly apparent in the multitude of tables and desks made specifically for women.

As Paris, with its mixture of aristocratic and bourgeois patrons, became the arbiter of taste, the importance of middle-men in forming fashion increased. Whereas the court employed craftsmen directly, ordinary mortals usually bought via the *marchand-merciers*, furniture dealers who often had interests in the making of furniture as well as in the retail aspects of the trade. They could show designs which would be made up in other people's companies.

Furniture making was a highly specialized business. The guild system of France was powerful, chock full of vested interests, and its members went in for demarcation disputes as recondite as those of their modern equivalents. A member of the cabinet-makers' guild could not collect mounts for his furniture from a member of the bronze-casters' guild. They had to be delivered by the caster.

The *menuisiers* were joiners, workers in solid wood mainly concerned with seat furniture. *Ébénistes* were cabinet-makers, at the center of whose craft lay the art of veneering. Carvers provided sculptural work. There was considerable jockeying for position between them and each jealously preserved his own speciality. They kept standards high by controlling the admission of new masters, by checking the quality of work produced and, after 1743, by insisting that each master stamp his work with his name or monogram as a guarantee of quality. Over the years son followed father into the ranks of the *menuisiers* or the *ébénistes*. Sometimes an outsider, taken on as a workman or apprentice, would

A gilt wood Louis XV *fauteuil* of c1750 with fine low cabriole legs and a delicately carved apron. The arms bend outwards at a slightly more extravagant angle than is usual. The tapestry seat and back follow the work of the painter Boucher, who designed for the Gobelins factory.

become a master and then gain an atelier by marrying into one of the furniture-making dynasties. Thus Riesener, one of the band of great German craftsmen attracted to Paris by the scope the city afforded, took over Oeben's workshop when he married his widow, who was daughter of one master *ébéniste*, sister of another and sister-in-law of two others.

Three groups of craftsmen worked outside the guild system. From the Middle Ages custom sanctioned the independence of some small areas of the capital from the jurisdiction of the guilds. Provincial furniture makers went their own way, which was, so far as style was concerned, in the same direction as their Parisian brethren but a few paces in the rear. At the top of the hierarchy of furniture makers were the craftsmen employed directly by the crown. The *Ébéniste du Roi* had workshops on royal premises and was subject to none of the restrictions imposed by the guilds. He could

employ his own bronze casters, gilders and any other craftsmen he wished, and if he wanted to turn his own hand to casting or designing mounts he could. Consequently he was able to design and supervise the construction of every element which went into the production of a piece of furniture. Riesener, to take one example of the benefit afforded by this freedom, when he became *Ébéniste du Roi*, designed mounts with concealed lugs and rods to replace the unsightly screw holes which disfigured earlier mounts. These resulted from the fact that a run of identical mounts was usually produced with no attention paid to specific use. Royal patronage alone, without the special position of *Ébéniste du Roi*, did not free the craftsmen from guild jurisdiction. Charles Cressent, the greatest *ébéniste* of the Regency and cabinet-maker to Phillippe d'Orléans, the Regent, was prosecuted for making his own mounts immediately the Regency came to an end in 1723. He continued to work for the Dukes of Orleans, who were members of the royal family, but even their protection could not prevent the guild fining him and seizing his work in 1723 and again in 1735 and 1745.

The furniture of the Regency constitutes a half-way

A chest-of-drawers by Cressent. This is one of the finest pieces of the cabinet-maker's art produced during the Régence. It has a wealth of ormolu mounts which Cressent probably designed himself and had made in his own workshops. The commode is made of oak veneered with kingwood. The top is of marble. The impassive mask in the center and the flying winged dragons on either side bring dignity and fantasy into a superb juxtaposition.

house between the Louis XIV style and the full Rococo of Louis XV and it overlaps the actual Regency at both ends. Financial considerations had made parquetry and marquetry veneers popular in place of *pietre dure* in the last years of Louis XIV. The fashionable world also began to prefer curved outlines for its furniture to the rectangularity of Louis XIV work. Both these elements were continued and developed under the Regency.

During the Regency and even more during the reign of Louis XV new types of furniture proliferated. The commode was the most important piece of container furniture and could be of the type known, suitably, as the *commode à la Régence* (or *en tombeau*) with three vertically arranged drawers mounted on short legs or the Louis XV commode with two or four drawers arranged in two layers and with longer legs. There were a number of slight variations on these two basic patterns. A major new commode form was the *encoignure* or corner cupboard, usually supplied in twos. In mid century the commode gained a pair of doors to enclose the whole front and was known as the *commode à vantaux*.

Table desks (*bureaux plats*) were popular, as were *secretaires*, particularly fall-front versions (*secretaires à abattant*), during the Louis XV period. Roll top desks (*bureaux à cylindre*) came into fashion at the end of the reign and were especially well liked in the following reign. It seems probable that the success of one piece of furniture was responsible for this fashion. The Bureau du Roi Louis XV, the roll-top desk begun by Oeben and finished by Riesener, and which may be the world's most famous piece of furniture, was so well received that similar pieces were demanded immediately by the fashionable world. Desks with a superstructure of small drawers continued to be produced but were more popular under Louis XIV and later, under the influence of Martin Carlin's work, in Louis XVI's time.

Tables were made for a multitude of specialized uses, including eating (under English influence. Surprisingly, the home of gastronomy did not usually build special rooms or furniture for eating until the 18th century). Other tables were made specially for reading, painting, holding soft craft materials — embroidery and needlework—and supporting candelabra. Many tables and desks stand witness to one of the rages of the 18th century. Everyone seems to have been fascinated with mechanical toys and contrivances. Ger-

The Tower Drawing room in Waddesdon Manor, England. The paneling of this octagonal room was made c1770–75 for a house in Issy, near Meudon, in France and was transported from there when Baron Ferdinand de Rothschild built Waddesdon in the 19th century. The roll-top desk, a superb piece of French cabinet-making, was made by Riesener c1773, probably for Mme Adelaide, one of Louis XV's daughters. The chairs are of the Louis XVI period and the firescreen was made c1780. The Savonnerie carpet is of c1754. The early 18th-century French chandelier is made of steel and rock crystal. The porcelain is Sèvres of the 1760s. The terracottas on the fireplace are late 18th century, by Clodion.

many had produced mechanical oddities for years and perhaps the influx of German craftsmen to Paris in the 18th century was partly responsible for desks and tables being equipped with mechanical means of transformation. Although they never reached the heights of absurdity of some multi-purpose patent furniture of the 19th century a number of pieces combine a fancifully heterogeneous collection of functions.

Under Louis XV the *marquise*, a double armchair, was developed, as were special chairs with swivel seats for use at the dressing table. The *voyeuse* was a chair with a wide, padded horizontal rail surmounting the back. It was supposedly for use by two people during games of cards. One sat and played, the other watched, leaning with his elbows on the rail. They may also have been used in the same way as the rather similarly structured English library chair, which was straddled by the user, who rested his open book on the rail. Probably the best known of 18th-century chairs is the *bergère*. Whereas the normal armchair had open sides under the arms, the *bergère* had back and sides closed with either upholstery or cane.

Daybeds (*chaises-longues*) had been in use for a hundred years before one end developed a back and sides like a *bergère* and became the *duchesse*. Sometimes the *duchesse* was in two pieces: one a small *bergère*, the other a long stool of the same height; sometimes three sections were used, in which case the stool had a low *bergère* at one end to form a foot, facing the *bergère* which constituted the head.

For all seat furniture cane seats and backs became fashionable in the Regency. Stretchers were still normally to be found on chairs, sofas and daybeds during the Regency, but disappeared completely in the Louis XV style. The cabriole leg, introduced from China in the 17th century, provided the basis for the typical outline of all Louis XV furniture. It is most obvious in seat furniture but the serpentine line of the Rococo mirrors it with its three-dimensional curves and reverse curves.

The age of Louis XV (1723–1774) is often called the age of Rococo. Rococo interior decoration, a fined-down version of the Baroque repertory of shells, waves, fronds, figures, fruit and flowers, originally sprang from the designs of Meissonnier and Pineau. It is a decoration applied to a flat surface, light, pleasing and essentially insubstantial. The furniture, however, gradually became more sculptural, the same motifs which

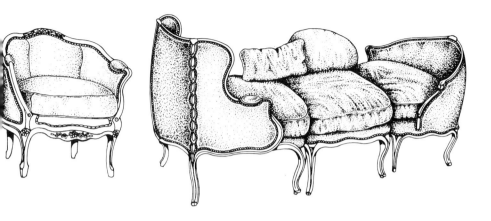

Three examples of seat furniture from the reign of Louis XV, a time when physical comfort became a central preoccupation of furniture makers. On the right is a well-upholstered chaise longue, in the center a *marquise* and, on the left, an example of a *bergère* with cabriole legs.

spread two-dimensionally across a flat wall being translated into three dimensions.

The Rococo love of lightness and frivolity ran side by side with a growth of interest in the exotic. Lacquer returned to popularity and grand pieces from the previous reign were broken up and their panels cut down and re-used. In 1730 Guillaume and Etiennne-Simon Martin were granted a monopoly of the production of imitation Chinese and Japanese lacquer in relief. However, they and their two brothers are better known for *vernis Martin*. This was a lustrous pseudo-lacquer, comprising as many as 40 coats of varnish, sometimes with a sprinkling of gold dust under the surface and made in a wide variety of colors. *Vernis Martin* was used for some of the loveliest furnishings of the period.

The Middle East as well as the Far East provided inspiration for Rococo furnishings. Upholstery became a far more important factor in creating the shape of seat furniture. Oval sofas were known as *ottomanes* and were fashionable under Louis XV and XVI. Marie Antoinette, at the end of the Louis XVI period, had a *boudoir turc* at Fontainebleau.

The Transitional style, Louis XVI and the Directory The Neoclassical style associated with the reign of Louis XVI started well before he ascended the throne in 1774. The appointment of the Marquis de Marigny, the brother of Mme de Pompadour, as *Surintendant des Bâtiments* in 1751, following a visit to Italy in the company of the Neoclassicist engraver and writer

Nicholas Cochin, is often seen as the beginning of court interest in reintroducing Classical forms for furniture.

Whereas the Classical elements in Louis XIV work provided visual metaphors for the power of the monarchy and of the monarch himself, the Neoclassicism of the end of Louis XV's reign and of that of Louis XVI was just another form of exoticism. It remained so until the Empire (1800–14), when moral and imperial meanings became dominant in the movement. However, the first great French work of Neoclassical interior decoration, Mme du Barry's furnishing of Louveciennes in 1771 owed nothing to any Caesar other than Louis XV, who, incidentally, was not much taken with the new style.

Although Rococo furnishings continued to be produced till the end of the Ancien Regime in 1789, the new style had superseded it by 1770 after a decade labeled "Transitional", during which the straight lines of Neoclassicism and the curves of Rococo combined in the same pieces of furniture or when Neoclassical decorations were applied to essentially Rococo forms.

In the 1770s outlines became rectangular again. Legs straightened and their straightness was emphasized by fluting or by ascending spirals. Ormolu was applied in bands or rectangles in which the Greek key pattern, paterae or interlinking circles were common features, although it was quite possible for Rococo swags of crinkled ribbon, birds and leaves to be used. Riesener was particularly fond of the wrinkled ribbon motif. In his jewel cabinet for the Comtesse de Provence, now in the British Royal Collection, the elements of Rococo decoration are exquisitely transmuted into a pattern of Neoclassical balance and repose by the use of mirror images on each side. This same piece is veneered in mahogany, the wood which, under English influence, became fashionable in the Neoclassical period, when veneers cut to show its fine figure or arranged into a diamond parquetry replaced detailed marquetry on many pieces. The lack of conflict between Neoclassical and Rococo styles between 1760 and 1790 can be gauged from the fact that an *ébéniste* could turn out commodes with floral marquetry and with plain veneers at the same time and any connoisseur would be happy to have both in the same room. In England King George IV combined the styles happily, from the 1780s and 1790s until well into the

A worktable by Weisweiler, c1780. This exquisite three-tiered worktable exemplifies the restraint of the best Neoclassical furniture of the Ancien Régime. The ormolu mounts and gilding are used to outline and emphasize the delicate diamond-shaped veneers, whose pattern is varied on the inside of the top tier by a series of interlocking circles. The plaques show the popularity of Wedgwood's blue jasper plaques in Europe in the 1780s. They are Sèvres made in imitation of Wedgwood.

19th century in the superb collections of French furniture which he formed in his palaces.

Painted Sèvres plaques and lacquer had been very popular in Rococo furniture and some *ébénistes* continued to use them up to the Revolution. Carlin and Weisweiler are the best known of this group. Imitations of Josiah Wedgwood's jasperware plaques were introduced as part of the fashion for things English in the 1780s, a fashion which ran through all things. Mme de la Tour du Pin recorded that by 1789, "Everything had to be copied from our neighbors, from the constitution to horses and carriages." Fashionable young men affected an English accent.

Despite the bankruptcy of the crown the court and the rich citizens of Paris continued to order furniture made from the most precious materials. Some of Weisweiler's furniture of the 1780s is exquisite enough to be more like jewelry than ordinary furniture and c1785 Riesener supplied the Queen with a roll-topped desk and work table veneered with mother-of-pearl and with mounts of gilt and silvered bronze. The two most famous of ormolu designers were at work in this period: Pierre Gouthière and Thomire. Gouthière invented the process by which mounts could be gilt, part matt and part gloss.

Besides Riesener, Weisweiler and Carlin, a list of the great *ébénistes* of the Louis XVI period would have to

Right: A commode by Riesener, dated 1780. It was made at the very end of the Transitional period; although the main shape, the marquetries and the mounts are all Neoclassical, the piece retains modified cabriole legs. The diamond-pattern marquetries of the drawer fronts are a common feature of Riesener's work. He often used rectangular mounts.

Left: A mid-18th-century *bonheur du jour*, a woman's writing desk, by Martin Carlin. Carlin often used Sèvres plaques in his pieces, particularly this kind of very delicate flower decoration. The end of the Rococo style is apparent in the very gentle curve of the legs.

include Dubois, Beneman, Molitor, Leleu, Stöckel. The names of *menuisiers* tend to be generally less well known than those of *ébénistes* but the age of Neoclassicism contains two exceptions; Sené and Georges Jacob. Jacob and his two sons dominated the furniture world of the Directoire and the Empire and Georges Jacob himself had considerable importance during the last years of Louis XVI. He introduced solid mahogany chairs from England and from 1785 onwards developed a more correct Classicism under the painter David's influence. The Directoire style owed much to both men, including the predominance of the saber-legged chair, imported from England, where it had been copied from the Greek *klismos*.

Directoire style is a more academic Classicism than that which preceded it. It is rather more theatrical than Louis XVI Classicism and takes itself a little too seriously, though not as seriously as the Empire was to do. The *méridienne*, a solid, sparsely upholstered day bed with curled decoration on the raised ends, the *athénienne*, a tripod-based free-standing wash-handstand, tripod candelabra, and vase stands, are the other best-known creations of the time. Work produced by others than the Jacobs or by the remaining cabinet-makers of the old order tended to be a little shoddy compared with contemporary English or German work. After the comfortable dignity and intimacy of the furniture of the 1770s and 1780s, the 1790s prepare us for the sham of furniture being given, in its Classical motifs, a moral significance which seems not only unnecessary but absurdly inappropriate.

England

After Henry VIII broke the English allegiance to the Papacy in 1531 Englishmen continued to travel to Italy, but the long tradition of Italian artists and craftsmen working in England was broken. They did not return until the 18th century. The main influence on English visual arts and on furniture came from Protestant Northern Europe, particularly from the Low Countries and some of the German states.

Through much of the 16th century the basic shapes of many pieces of furniture remained Medieval with Renaissance ornament applied to them. Under Henry VIII (1509–47) Romayne work, carved roundels enclosing profile heads, was popular. The Medieval habit of gilding and painting furniture continued. During the course of the 16th century carving in the round for table legs and cupboard supports became increasingly popular. For grand furniture heraldic beasts were a common subject for supports.

In the Elizabethan period (1558–1603) strapwork, a flat geometrical decoration usually carved in low relief, was adapted from the Low Countries. Cabochons, raised oval ornaments, were often incorporated within the strapwork design. Bed posts and table legs

Louis XV (1723–74)

Armchairs developed cabriole legs in Régence period (1715–23); now lost their stretchers. Upholstery became more comfortable.

Flowing lines and extreme delicacy mark the best of Rococo.

Louis XVI (1774–91)

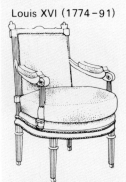

Even ornate armchairs adopt straight legs and geometrical form. Ornament is regular. Comfort comes from deep seat cushions.

From the 1740s until the end of the century first Rococo (Louis XV) and then a delicate Neoclassicism (Louis XVI) dominated the French decorative arts. In both periods lacquer panels were used, multi-colored under Louis XV, usually black and gold under Louis XVI. Swirling lines and cabriole legs were usual under Louis XV, straight lines and legs under Louis XVI. Rococo is essentially asymmetrical, Neoclassicism symmetrical. During the Rococo, fine floral marquetries were popular. In the Neoclassical period apart from string banding, plain veneers were preferred. Gilding was common throughout.

Mounts and keyhole escutcheons Rococo in asymmetrical flowing lines.

During Louis XV's reign beds in alcoves became popular.

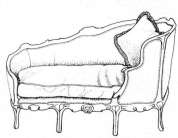

Asymmetricality of the *veilleuse* and its deep cushions was Rococo in nature.

Mounts and keyhole surrounds regular and restrained in shape.

Legs became straight, wooden veneers plain. Gilt–bronze mounts were arranged symmetrically.

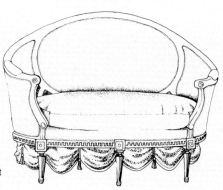

Ottomans show love of the exotic, but even this is tamed. Symmetry prevails.

TUDOR AND STUART

sprouted enormous bulbs, reaching a dropsical size in the 1580s and 1590s and becoming smaller in the Jacobean period (1603–c40). Inlaying was carried out but much less expertly than in France or Italy. Box, ebony and holly were among the woods employed. Although through the 16th and much of the 17th century oak was the wood most frequently used, the Elizabethans started to use beech, walnut and chestnut for some fine furniture.

Seat furniture in the Early Tudor period (c1485–c1547) changed little from its Medieval precursors. Stools and benches were the common forms of seating, though joined and turned chairs were more generally used. Also widely found was the bench table, which had a hinged back so that it could be transformed from bench back to table top. They all continued to be made up to and during the Commonwealth of 1649–60. Settles were often fixed to the floor or to the wall.

The first English chairs without arms were made c1600. They are called farthingale chairs since it is thought they were developed to allow a woman wearing a farthingale to sit comfortably. They can be of two sorts: both have a low back; both are often upholstered on back and seat with turkey work, which is upholstery that imitates Turkey carpets. But whereas one has a normal flat seat, the other, which is usually taller, has a sloping seat and is found only in very wealthy homes. It was made so that female courtiers could rest and yet appear to be standing, in the same way that monks used misericord seats during long church services. Early in the 17th century the three-legged stool was superseded by the four-legged joined stool.

Tables dormants, frame tables on fixed supports, had appeared in the 14th century, and came into wide use when a room was set aside specifically for eating. However, trestle tables continued to be used as dining tables for servants through the 16th and early 17th centuries. In the second half of the 16th century draw-tables with pull-out leaves were invented for dining and a small dropleaf table joined the games tables (which had compartments for dice) which had been produced earlier in the century. The gate-leg table was created in the middle of the 17th century.

Open cupboards for the display of plate continued in use from Medieval times and in the late 16th century became the three-tiered open court cupboard which

The Great Bed of Ware, c1580, a particularly ornate version of the English bed as designed between 1550 and 1600. The back posts of the earlier part of the century have been superseded by a heavily carved headboard which supports the tester at one end. In this bed the ordinary bulb posts at the foot have been replaced by posts with architectural bases, urns and complexly carved columns. Lion masks, volutes and acanthus scrolls reflect the influence of the Classical revival in England, more obvious in literature than in the visual arts.

was often elaborately carved and set with semi-precious stones. Aumbries and livery cupboards were used for food storage, press cupboards which were tall and often had shelves inside were used for clothes and valuables. Joined chests replaced plank chests in the course of the 16th century and before 1600 the mule chest, which had a pull-out drawer in the base, had been developed. About 1650 the chest-of-drawers appeared. Nonesuch chests are a late 16th-century speciality. They are decorated with a marquetry picture or pictures of an exotic building wrongly thought to have been Henry VIII's Palace of Nonesuch, destroyed in the 17th century.

Through the 16th and 17th centuries beds were the most important and valuable pieces of furniture, prized less for the materials of which the bedstead was made than for their hangings and bedding. The early 16th-century bed had a tester (wooden canopy) suspended from the ceiling. By the mid-century this had been

143

TUDOR AND STUART

Left: A court cupboard of c1610, which shows the English taste for sturdy oak furniture. In the Jacobean period both levels of court cupboards were usually open; here both are enclosed and the bulbs and pillars of the upper part are vestigial remains kept as decoration. The design on the upper frieze derives from Tudor strapwork.

Right: A Stuart chair and an Elizabethan court cupboard from Melford Hall, England. The decoration of the front splat of the chair is Dutch influenced. The elaboration of the pierced carving of the back is unusual, but it has the typical tall thin proportions of post-Restoration chairs. The court cupboard, of oak, is very elaborately carved. It contains a mixture of religious and secular motifs: terms and swags of fruit derive from Classical or pagan sources; angels carrying souls up to heaven (on the side doors) are Christian.

replaced by the four poster. In the second half of the century the four poster was often replaced by a bed whose canopy rested on two posts at the foot but on an enormous and elaborately carved headboard at the other end. By the 1620s iron bedsteads could be found but they were far less common than oak ones. An inventory of the furniture of Gainsborough Old Hall in Lincolnshire in 1625 mentions an iron bed and specifies that another bedstead was made of cypress wood. However, the main concentration in the list is on the accurate description of bed hangings. Taffeta or turkey work seem to have been respectively the great luxury and the more usual good material for bed hangings.

Materials continued as essential furnishings. Tapestry and turkey work offset the rather gloomy appearance of the linenfold paneling common to Tudor interiors.

In general the Commonwealth was marked by grea-

ter simplicity in its furnishings than the period which preceded it. Ornament was kept to a minimum, though some great houses, such as Wilton House in Wiltshire were being furnished at that time and if the furniture matched the style of the interior decoration it must have been magnificent. Unfortunately, little fine furniture of the period remains.

In 1660 the monarchy was restored and Charles II became king. His years of exile in France and Holland gave him a more intimate acquaintance with foreign furnishings than that of any previous king. Louis XIV was already turning his court into the center of European fashion; the luxury of his surroundings appealed to Charles II as a model for his own. Besides the French and Dutch influences an exotic element was added by the arrival of Catherine of Braganza as Charles' wife. She brought Portuguese furniture with her, some

An ebonized silver-mounted table, c1670. Such grand furniture was made for display rather than use. The silver plaques on the table top stand proud of the wood and create a hazard for anything, glass or cup, placed on the table. The center plaque bears the initials of Elizabeth, Countess of Dysart.

A painted Stuart hall chair. The Italian parentage of the set of chairs of which this is a member is very clear from the solid front and back sections which take the place of legs and are pierce carved. The shell which forms the back is a common Baroque motif. Such chairs were used by footmen in attendance in an anteroom. This form was rarely seen in England.

workmanship from the Portuguese trading center of Goa and a fine collection of Chinese and Japanese lacquer. The furnishings of the court and the houses of the great nobles reflect this exotic mixture, but the large middle class and the more stay-at-home members of the aristocracy continued to use and order furniture even towards the end of the 17th century which would not have been out of place in a Jacobean interior. The revocation in 1685 of the Edict of Nantes (which had safeguarded the rights of Protestants) brought a flood of French Huguenot refugees to England, including craftsmen. They increased French influence on English work just as the arrival of William of Orange as King of England in 1688 increased Dutch influence.

The most luxurious furniture of the late 17th century was of silver; usually sheets of repoussé silver were shaped over an oak carcase but sometimes the whole piece was cast in solid metal. Two suites of silver furniture survive in the Royal Collection at Windsor Castle: one set in solid cast silver presented to William of Orange by the City of London, one in silver over oak presented by the city to Charles II. More common was ebony or ebonized furniture decorated with repoussé silver plaques. A number of fine Baroque cabinets and tables exist in this style, the Baroque having been introduced from Italy by the French and the Dutch. Gilding was popular but silvering more so, particularly

A japanned chair, English, c1675. The back splat is curved to the curve of the body for greater comfort. The legs are unusual for their sidewards turning feet. Although the japanned scenes are vaguely oriental, no attempt has been made to pretend that this is an oriental piece.

A late 17th-century lacquered cabinet-on-stand. The superstructure and stand are of silvered wood, more popular in the late 17th-century than gilded work. Birds were a common motif as were swags of flowers. The legs are more complicated than usual, though stretchers forming a pattern were quite common. The flat heads in the center of each set of stretchers probably originally supported a vase.

for cabinet stands which were sculpted in the round.

Equal to the love of silver furniture was the passion for lacquer which swept England. The Portuguese and the Dutch had a thriving trade with the Far East and the English East India company imported porcelain and lacquer. At first it was referred to as "India work" or "Coromandel work" since the East India Company acquired it from the traders of the Coromandel coast in India.

In time the true sources of lacquer in China and Japan were realized. Since Japanese lacquer was the more highly prized, lacquer became known as "japan", and the process of its imitation in the West, "japanning". In 1688 John Stalker and George Parker wrote *A Treatise of Japanning and Varnishing* which gives instructions for making and decorating japanned work, for use by professional furniture makers and by the amateur public which had taken to japanning as a hobby.

To turn lacquer into "well made" pieces three methods

were employed: European pieces were sent out to the East to be lacquered; European craftsmen traveled there to make pieces for lacquering; and oriental screens were imported and the panels cut up and reassembled by European cabinet-makers. Screen patterns, which frequently include Chinese symbols like the "precious objects" or the "emblems of happy augury", were misunderstood. In consequence screens were often cut up in such a way that the panels, when fitted together to form a cabinet, present an incongruous juxtaposition of scenes or parts of scenes. Stalker and Parker argued against such absurdities as mutilating scenes so that men are shown "chasing the Boar in the middle of the Ocean".

Although silver and lacquer were the most luxurious materials used for fine furniture, probably the most important introduction into English cabinet-making in the late 17th century was the refined art of marquetry. Marquetry had developed from the early 17th-century art of inlay in France, Italy and the Low Countries. At the Restoration, and later with the flood of Huguenot refugees and the Dutch followers of William of Orange, the techniques of overlaying pieces with a fine veneer of many woods were developed in England. Walnut was frequently used for the carcase although oak was also quite common. Laburnum branches supplied the oyster pattern marquetry which was exceptionally popular in England. Holly, ebony, satinwood and purplewood recur in cabinet decoration. An inlay of engraved, and sometimes dyed, ivory was often combined with the veneering.

From Holland England gained a taste for floral marquetry. Sometimes the pattern is of flowers and leaves alone but more often they are represented in a vase or stand. Another popular form was arabesque marquetry, an overall intricate pattern of tight swirling lines distantly descended from Islamic decorative motifs, which probably came into England from Portugal or from Spain via the Low Countries. Endive or seaweed marquetry which, as its names suggest, was a pattern built up from small, frond-like ornaments, was also much employed.

As usual modified versions of the furniture made for the great became available to a wider public. Daniel Marot, the architect who accompanied William III to England, is credited with introducing the distinctive William and Mary chair shape. This developed from the

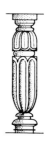

Three popular forms of turned and carved supports from the 17th century. From top, bobbin turning, double cup, fluted baluster.

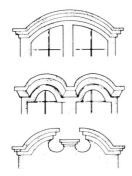

Three cornice shapes fashionable in the very early 18th century.

more conventionally shaped (in terms of seat height) walnut armchair of the Charles II period. It had short, turned back legs, cabriole front legs, low seat and tall thin back with a carved top. A succession of materials became popular at court for seat furniture and spread rapidly to the country. Walnut was popular from the time of Charles II onwards. At the Restoration cane was introduced for seats, for small panels inset in the backs of chairs and as the base for a mattress on daybeds. By the end of the reign (1685) cane had come to be ousted by stuffed upholstery for armchairs and by wood with a cushion or by a small panel of stuffed upholstery for upright chairs. Armchairs became common in the houses of the ordinary middle class by the end of the 17th century.

During the reign of Queen Anne (1702–14) an English mode of furnishing emerged from which the Georgian style was to develop. The foreign-inspired marquetry of the Restoration and of William and Mary was simplified so that the beauty of an object, be it cabinet, chest-of-drawers, bookcase or bureau, depended primarily on the basic shape of the object and the beauty of the figuring of the walnut chosen for an all-over veneer. The only marquetry elements which were generally maintained were string and feather banding (strips of wood, the grain running across the width) whose purpose was to define the area of veneer covering each door or drawer panel. The cabriole leg which had appeared in the previous reign lost its stretchers and often gained a delicately carved shell at the knee. Comfort and quiet dignity mark the style associated with the name of the domestically minded Anne, who, as the poet Pope pointed out, did "sometimes Counsel take and sometimes tea".

In the early Georgian period (1714–c1735) there are two distinct lines of development in fine English furniture. The domestic style of Queen Anne was continued. Lines became more serpentine. The shape of the cabriole leg was carried through in the back splat of a chair and the claw and ball foot was produced. Like the cabriole leg this probably had a Chinese origin. Walnut was dominant. The impression created in the middle-class room or in that belonging to the large class of local gentry was of quiet dignity.

The second line of development reflected the results of the 18th-century devolution of power to the great landed nobles. This wealthy caste developed a taste for

EARLY GEORGIAN

Left: An early Georgian chair of c1725, made of walnut and walnut veneer. The cabriole leg was introduced during the reign of Queen Anne, but whereas then it had a plain leg, pad feet and, at the most, a small shell decoration at the knee, by the Georgian period it had gained complex acanthus and shield carving rising over the bottom of the seat rail. The claw and ball foot was introduced. The top rail is finely carved and the back splat elegantly shaped.

Right: A William Kent writing table, one of a pair made in gilt mahogany c1735 for Devonshire House, England. The lion-headed terms and the roundels show Kent's indebtedness to Classical inspiration. His taste in furnishing inclined to a restrained Baroque. Here he uses the seashell motif.

the rich Baroque furnishings fashionable in Europe. When not in London on parliamentary business each major political family virtually held its own court in the palaces they built for themselves throughout England. In those palaces, such as Chatsworth in Derbyshire and Houghton Hall in Norfolk, the furniture continued the tradition of European courts in its use of gilt, of sculptural members and of Italian velvets for bed hanging.

Marot also produced designs for beds. These brought a French/Dutch Baroque splendor into English design in which draperies played an important part. Sometimes the front posts of the bed disappeared altogether and the tester was suspended from above. It was crowned with ostrich plumes or with carved swags and trophies covered in velvet and great swags of drap-

The dining room from Nostell Priory, England. The room dates from the George II period, although Robert Adam altered some of the decorations later on. The dining chairs are George II. The side table is by Chippendale to a design by Paine, the architect of the house, who also designed some of the furniture. The great oil lamps are from the end of the 18th century. The dining table is 19th century. The keynote of the furniture is simple, masculine elegance, and its comfort reflects the importance of the dining room in the social and political life of a man of position in 18th-century England.

155

A chest-of-drawers ascribed to Channon, c1785. The complexity of its shape is more associated with Netherlandish work, though it is more restrained. The top is of wood and the surrounds of gilt bronze. The bottom motifs are of agile dolphins, the handles and keyhole surrounds are in the leaf and flame motifs of Rococo. The heads are finely sculpted.

ery hung from it. Elaborately carved mermen or caryatids at the bedhead support carved and gilt draperies to form a grandiose headboard. Some 20 years later (c1722), William Kent is thought to have designed the bed in the Green State Bedroom at Houghton Hall in Norfolk. The bed-head consists of two superimposed gilded shells carved above a gilded architectural pediment. The bed-curtains and tester are of green velvet, with a gold fringe to the tester. The bed-coverings are of gold velvet.

Kent's side-tables, usually of carved and gilded wood with marble tops, are in the full Baroque tradition. His desks often include the great shell motif of Baroque art. The impression he gives is of vibrant life, solidity, permanence and grandeur. There is nothing reticent about Kent.

A number of furniture makers carried out important commissions in the late 17th and early 18th centuries. Gerreit Jensen produced fine marquetry in the Boulle style in tortoiseshell, brass and pewter. John Gumley and James Moore were in partnership and supplied the court, amongst other clients, with looking glasses and gilt furniture.

After Kent's work the Rococo style gradually became fashionable. It was adapted from France by English goldsmiths years before it was thought suitable for

A Chippendale library table. Thomas Chippendale the Elder supplied this piece to Nostell Priory, England, in 1767, though it was completed the year before. The lion-headed and footed terms, the garlands and oval decorations are carved in solid mahogany.

furniture. In 1744 Matthias Lock published six designs for mirrors and in 1746 followed them with six designs for tables. Mirror frames were the responsibility of the carver and it was through carving that the Rococo found acceptance. The S scroll, curves and an asymmetrical approach to decorative clusters of fruit, flowers and birds began to be approved. During the 1740s and 1750s in England fantasy was seen as a desirable quality in furniture. French Rococo came into its own. Channon, a London cabinet-maker, produced c1750 a group of desks whose serpentine curved mahogany fronts and corners are embellished with Rococo gilt bronzes, brass mounts and handles. The Gothic came into vogue. Strawberry Hill, Horace Walpole's little house at Twickenham, began to be decorated in Gothic style in 1749. Matthias Lock and Copland introduced Chinoiserie in their *A New Book of Ornament* of 1752. In 1751 Matthew Darly was responsible for *A New Book of Chinese, Gothic and Modern Chairs.*

An alternative kind of fantasy was served by the appearance of so-called rustic furniture. In 1751–52 William and John Halfpenny published their designs in *Rural Architecture in the Chinese Taste.* Its title reveals

the confusion of the back-to-nature movement with Chinese art. The belief that there was a truth to be discovered in simplicity and country life was mirrored in the supreme artifice of weaving chairs and tables from simulated boughs to form the furniture for a "simple" summerhouse.

All these fantasy forms are elements in the work of Thomas Chippendale the Elder. He was born in Otley, Yorkshire, in 1718, the son of a joiner. His career is not particularly well documented, but by 1753 he had a thriving business in St Martin's Lane in London, the center of the English furniture business. In 1754 he published the first edition of his *"Gentleman and Cabinet-Maker's Directory"*. It reveals the work of a man who was not a great innovator but whose work, the first devoted entirely to furniture, represents the greatest compilation of the variety of furniture designs available at one period. The unselfconscious juxtaposition of Rococo, Gothic and Chinoiserie is striking, as is the readiness to modify patterns. Alternative decorations are often given on each side of a drawing of a chair, bed or table. The book is blatantly an advertising

Above: A Chippendale ribbon-back chair, more frequently seen with claw and ball feet. This is a very elaborate version, particularly in the leg carving.

Above left: A Chippendale ladder-back chair, one of the simplest and most often produced designs from Chippendale's workshop. It is elegant and practical. Chippendale's devotion to detail can be seen in the modulation and articulation of the ladder slats.

Above: A Chippendale Chinese-back chair. The main identifying feature of Chinese Chippendale is the geometrical arrangement of rectangles and triangles in the back. The legs are usually, as here, of square section.

Above right: A Chippendale Gothic chair, more restrained than some. The four Early English arches in the back, with their broken trefoil tracery, derive from Gothic architecture.

journal put out by a tradesman. It was aimed at potential customers whose wants and whims would be catered for and it was aimed at other tradesmen to make them *au fait* with what was happening in the metropolis.

So much furniture was at one time ascribed to Chippendale that it has become impossible to dissociate his name from almost any fairly ornate Rococo English work, particularly chairs, of the mid-18th century. In fact his firm made an astonishing variety of furnishings and he was clearly an entrepreneur and businessman of something like genius. The St Martin's Lane workshops turned out quantities of much plainer, cheaper furniture than that usually meant when the phrase "Chippendale style" is used. The common denominator of both cheap and expensive furniture is that most of it was in mahogany.

Mahogany had been imported in small quantities to England from San Domingo and Cuba in the 17th century. Following France's embargo on the export of French walnut when disease destroyed walnut trees in France in 1720 England increased the import of

159

mahogany to help remedy the shortage of suitable furniture timber. Its rich color and close texture lent themselves to the handsome carved furniture popular among the wealthy.

An interesting insight into Chippendale's position, part tradesman, part artist, part supplier is revealed by the records of his work at Nostell Priory in Yorkshire where his firm worked for Sir Rowland Winn. Furniture made for the house included writing tables, desks, clothes presses, chairs, mirror frames, picture frames, dressing tables, games tables, commodes, stools, sofas, beds and even a barometer case. Some of the work is in French Rococo style, some in Chinese style, including a gilt pier glass surmounted by decoration of a Chinese garden pavilion and fabulous birds. Some shows the strong influence of English Classicism and some is as plain as work produced under the early Georges (1714–60). Chippendale's firm supplied curtains, hung wallpaper and laid carpets, and like any other tradesman he was berated, by letter at least, when deliveries were late.

Chippendale was always open to new ideas and influences. In 1762 the great Scottish architect Robert Adam started to influence fashionable taste towards the Neoclassical in furniture design. That same year the third edition of Chippendale's *Gentleman's and Cabinet-Maker's Directory* appeared and in it he added a few Neoclassical pieces to his repertory. During the 1760s Adam designed interiors in the Roman style. The most famous is probably the ante-room at Syon House where the decoration consists of gilded trophies of war, green marble columns dredged from the Tiber, gilded statues and marble-topped, gilded side-tables. During the 1770s decoration became paler and more delicate: pastel shades were used. Carpets were woven with patterns reflecting the paint and plaster decorations of the ceiling and fixed furniture, side-tables and mirrors, were designed as integral parts of the decoration of the room. Adam worked at Nostell Priory and Harewood House in Yorkshire in the 1760s and 1770s – as did Chippendale. Probably under Adam's influence Chippendale introduced into his work a delicate marquetry using urns, swags of husks, lions' heads, in short the Neoclassical repertory of images, worked in mahogany, satinwood and other veneers. However, he continued to produce and supply furniture which is Rococo or which applies Neoclassical

A medal cabinet by Vile, the Royal Cabinet-Maker, made originally for George II and altered by Vile in 1760. It is of mahogany, with a satinwood veneer. The carving, in solid mahogany, is of exceptionally high quality.

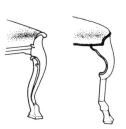

ornament to a basically Rococo piece. At Nostell in 1766 and 1771 he supplied respectively a writing table and dressing table whose outlines are as Rococo as if they had come from Louis XV's France. At the same house in 1769 he supplied a Pembroke games table with no Rococo features at all. It has straight legs and its only decoration is the rosewood banding around the dominant veneer of mahogany. In 1770 however, he produced a commode which combines a serpentine Rococo shape with a veneer of marquetry using urns and swags of husks.

For many years Chippendale's name overshadowed those of his contemporaries. However, the designs of Thomas Johnson in the Chinese taste have now been published and John Linnel's probable responsibility for the extraordinary Chinese bed from Badminton House (previously ascribed to Chippendale) has been advanced. Above all the quality of work ascribed to John Channon and that of William Vile and John Cobb—who were employed by King George II—has been recognized. One of the pieces by Vile and Cobb is possibly the finest example of carved and veneered case furniture of the English 18th century. This was the jewel cabinet for Queen Charlotte in mahogany and engraved ivory, supplied in 1761. Her accounts show a remarkable continuation of the old custom by which bed hangings and covers were far more valuable than the wooden frame. In 1762 Vile and Cobb supplied a special state bed to Queen Charlotte. The woodwork cost £205, other materials £380 and the lace counterpane a staggering £2,699.

For 20 years, from c1770 until his death in 1792, Robert Adam's style was the major influence on design. His architecture and furniture designs in the Neoclassical style brought about a revolution in the appearance of the English interior. Matthew Boulton in Birmingham produced ormolu mounts in the Classical style, Wedgwood plaques of draped Grecian figures graced furniture in England and France. Legs of chairs and tables became straight. Graeco/Roman ornament (misnamed Etruscan) was the only permissible form of ornament in any fashionable house.

Adam had studied in Italy. His journey there was not unusual, since many Englishmen in the 18th century completed their education by extensive traveling on the continent and particularly in Italy; and came back loaded with paintings and antiques. Adam knew well

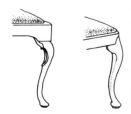

Four examples of 18th-century curved chair legs.

the world of the aristocratic politicians of the time who were also scholars and connoisseurs. Being a member of their society he mirrored their tastes and knew their priorities. He understood the importance of the dining room in English life. "The eating rooms are considered as the apartments of conversation, in which we pass a great deal of our time," he wrote. The elegant sideboard with its flanking urns on pedestals, ingeniously fitted to hold the necessities of a dining room is an Adam invention. He continued to use mahogany for the dining room, a strongly male preserve in the 18th-century house since the men usually remained there for some hours after the withdrawal of the women at the end of the evening meal. The furniture there is elegant but sturdy. In contrast drawing (or "withdrawing") rooms naturally tended to be given a feminine lightness and delicacy in their furnishings. In them satinwood and marquetry *bonheurs-du-jour* (little work-tables) were translated into an English idiom.

Two great names are linked with the Adam style and its development: George Hepplewhite and Thomas Sheraton. Little is known about them though it is known that like Chippendale they were born, brought up and learnt their trade in the provinces before gravitating to London. Hepplewhite was apprenticed to perhaps the greatest English provincial furniture-making house, Gillow of Lancaster. By 1760 he had a workshop in London but was little regarded until two years after his death in 1786 when his widow published the *Cabinet-Maker and Upholsterer's Guide.* This was so popular that a second edition was required in 1789. The most famous edition is the third of 1794 to which his widow added previously unpublished material. The book omits novelty furniture and concentrates on fine form and details of high quality craftsmanship. Though his firm produced a wide variety of furniture using other woods and other patterns, Hepplewhite's name is invariably linked with satinwood and with the shield-back chair. Other chair backs were square with an oval or slightly pedimented top. The backs contained struts, of which many forms exist, but of which the Prince of Wales feathers, the urn and the triple lilies are probably the best known. Legs are usually straight, of either round or square cross-section but he recommends a delicately modulated version of the cabriole leg for a three-legged music stool. The Hepplewhite sofa derived from the French sofa, but the

The bed-chamber from Osterley Park, England, dated 1776. This is one of the most spectacular beds designed by Robert Adam. The masses of drapery depend from a gilded tester which has sphinxes at the corners of the lower square section. The whole ensemble is crowned by gilded finials over an upper circular section. There is a gilt design on the bedhead, and the columns carry rows of painted bell-flowers.

curve of the back was usually more restrained, forming a long, delicate sweep of polished wood to frame the upholstery. Carved, japanned and painted furniture reappear in Hepplewhite. Painting was especially used and was to be even more used by Sheraton. Hepplewhite's dining furniture followed Adam's, particularly in the arrangement of sideboard and urns. The marquetry decoration became slightly more elaborate and included woods which were just being imported; thuyawood, zebrawood and amboyna as well as the mahogany, rosewood and satinwood already in use.

Sheraton's was a disappointed life. So far as is known he did not make a single piece of furniture, although he understood the technical requirements of craftsmanship. He lived and died in poverty and towards the end became mad. He scraped a living as a drawing master; his most important work, *The Cabinet-Maker and Upholsterer's Drawing Book*, was published in parts between 1791 and 1794 and it is on this

Above: A Sheraton chair. The Prince of Wales' feathers motif is associated with Hepplewhite but was used by Sheraton too. The shape is similar to designs in his "Cabinet-maker and Upholsterer's Drawing Book".

Above left: A Hepplewhite armchair. It has a shield back with Prince of Wales' feathers, and is a most elegant design.

that his reputation rests. Like Adam, Sheraton believed mahogany to be appropriate to the dining room. For chairs he approved mainly of square backs, completed in a large variety of ways with upright splats. These could be in mahogany or, for relative cheapness and lightness, in painted or japanned beech. Satinwood remained recommended for the drawing room and caning was thought useful for the seats of sofas. The Pembroke table as developed by Sheraton is extremely elegant. It invariably has two tiny drop-leaves which usually turn the table top into an oval when extended. Often it is painted or inlaid with shapes, ovals and swags of husk and bell-flower ornament. The legs are usually straight and placed conventionally one at each corner but pedestal and tripod variations are found. Sheraton delighted in designing ingenious dwarf cabinets fitted out with tiny drawers for writing imple-

A Sheraton worktable, the fine satinwood, cross-banding and inlays displaying the best of his style. The legs are delicate but just stop short of being spindly compared to the weight they have to support. The small circular handles frame a metal mount decorated with a simple Prince of Wales' feathers design.

SCANDINAVIA

ments. Desks and worktables often carried a low brass balustrade round part of the top to prevent objects rolling off. Beds returned to the four-post type. Washstands, usually in mahogany, were now supplied as open corner cupboards in bedrooms and their three legs make them reminiscent of the French *athénienne* of the same period.

Sheraton's later designs show an overelaboration which possibly stemmed from his mental degeneration. The elegance began to give way to ostentation.

Scandinavia

Very little is known about Scandinavian furniture until the 17th century since except in Jutland, where oak was sometimes used, Scandinavia lacked hardwoods and the soft deal and pine used to make furniture has not survived. By the 17th century political events ensured that the products of Sweden, Denmark and Norway would have strong similarities.

The three countries were united under the crown of Denmark from 1397 until 1433 when Sweden revolted. Denmark attempted to regain control but never succeeded. Norway remained joined to Denmark until 1814. German influence in Scandinavia was ensured by the cession of Schleswig and Holstein to Denmark in 1523 and by the Swedish involvement in the Thirty Years' War.

Yet the major discernible influence on Scandinavian furniture apparent even in the earliest remaining 17th-century pieces was the result not of political circumstances but of trade. A mixed English, Dutch and German ancestry can be seen in work produced in Sweden and Denmark in the mid- to late-17th century. A late 17th-century double-doored cupboard in the castle of Skokloster in Sweden which has drawers below and bun feet may be Swedish or North German. Contemporary veneered cupboards show French influence, chairs were mostly copied from English models, themselves often inspired by Dutch work.

Anglo-Dutch influence was increased by the enormous growth in trade between Norway and England after the Great Fire of London in 1666 and English influence on Sweden grew as did her mercantile expansion in the 18th century. Norway and Sweden were England's main suppliers of timber and iron ore respectively. Considerable quantities of English furniture were exported in return. By the early 18th century the

Early Georgian; the cabriole leg often ended with a claw and ball foot and with a shell delicately carved at the knee.

English Chinoiserie combined exotic birds, Chinese pavilions and C scrolls with plant and free forms.

Adam's Neoclassicism established urns as wine coolers.

18th-CENTURY ENGLAND

English furniture of the Queen Anne and Early Georgian periods (c1702–1740) continued to use walnut as the most important wood. Although the cabriole leg was introduced, lines remained simple. The beauty of the furniture depended on fine proportions, finely figured wood and expert joinery. By the 1740s mahogany was popular and the Rococo was introduced but it was usually more restrained than on the continent except in the most extravagant designs of Chippendale and Thomas Johnson. Gothic and Chinese designs were popular at the same time, until Adam re-established Neoclassicism as the dominant English style in the late 1760s and 1770s. This was the basis of English design until after the end of the century.

Broken pediment tops for case furniture were popular from the 1730s.

Chippendale Gothic chairs usually have ogee arches and quatrefoils in the tracery of the back. Legs often pierced.

End of the 18th century; furniture was simple, delicate and often of exquisite satinwood.

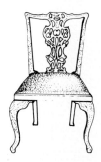

Chippendale Rococo chairs usually have cabriole legs, claw and ball feet and a pierced back splat.

Chippendale's Chinese chairs have geometrical designs, often including Rococo flourishes.

Hepplewhite straight chair legs replaced Rococo curves. The shield back was exten-sively used often incor-porating an urn or Prince of Wales feathers.

DENMARK AND NORWAY

Swedes referred to native chair makers who used cane seating as "English chair-makers."

Denmark and Norway remained remarkably conservative as far as chair-construction was concerned. A version of the upright William and Mary chair with cane back surrounded by a carved oak frame, cane seat and fancily carved front stretcher, continued to be made well into the 18th century. Basically early Georgian armchairs with a padded back, carved cresting, a pierce-carved front stretcher and claw and ball feet continued to be produced in Norway and Denmark until the 1760s. From 1746 to 1768 under pressure from the chair-makers' guild the government of Denmark prohibited the import of foreign chairs, so earlier styles were perpetuated. A form of Rococo decoration filtered through, however, and incongruously asymmetrical flourishes are found as crestings on otherwise ordinary Georgian chairs.

Much Scandinavian case-furniture of the first half of the 18th century shows a Dutch/German influence in its use of *bombé* shapes. These are far less pronounced, however, than in Dutch work. Even the English-inspired bureau-bookcase was often given a *bombé* base.

In the second half of the 18th century French influence replaced English, particularly for court furniture in both Copenhagen and Stockholm. Large quantities of French furniture were imported and Scandinavian craftsmen copied or emulated them. Georg Haupt, the Swedish cabinet-maker best known outside Sweden, was trained in Paris and London and the furniture he made in the Transitional and Louis XVI styles in Sweden in the 1770s bears comparison with Parisian work of the same period. Nils Dahlin, who worked in Stockholm in the 1760s, 1770s and 1780s was also probably trained in Paris. The quality of his ormolu mounts is excellent.

Dutch floral marquetry was popular in both courts in the early years of the 18th century but was replaced by a French-inspired marquetry, using musical instruments, books, or figures in the 1770s.

In the 1740s and 1750s Rococo became the court style as it did throughout Europe. It seems, however, to have had little effect in Scandinavia outside court circles. Scandinavia still possessed a large and, in, some cases, rich peasantry, whose furniture had probably changed little since the 16th century. In common with

Top right: A Danish chair made sometime between 1775 and 1785. This form of Neoclassical chair was made in both Denmark and Sweden. Compared to the finest French work of the period the proportions are a fraction crude.

Bottom right: A late 18th-century chair which closely follows English fashion. It was made by a Danish chairmaker who had studied his craft in England.

Bottom left: A Danish chair made c1767–68. It combines the shape of a contemporary English chair with a specifically Danish pattern on the back splat, the cipher of King Christian VII.

Top left: A Norwegian oak armchair of the early 18th century. It is in the English style, though the carved front splat is typically Scandinavian. The upholstery is gilt leather.

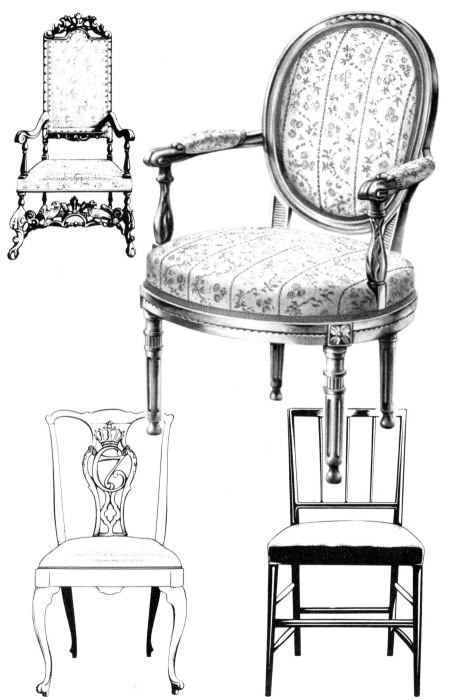

SCANDINAVIA

the furniture of Eastern Europe it was usually of deal or pine, painted either with a simple all-over color or with stylized patterns. Its simplicity of form may have prepared the way for the rapid assimilation of English Neoclassicism at its most straightforward by those people outside the court who bought furniture.

The Royal Furniture Emporium was set up in Copenhagen in 1777 to promote good design by Danish craftsmen. In 1781 its direction was given to the anglophile Carsten Anker. Danish and Norwegian craftsmen studied the new styles of Sheraton and Hepplewhite as soon as they appeared, but often reduced the forms to their bare essentials. A distant but original cousin of English work developed which, especially in Denmark, was remarkable for good craftsmanship and utmost economy of line. Stretchers and back staves were turned. Mahogany replaced walnut as the most fashionable wood and thin, strong turned members were made. The chairs produced in late 18th-century Denmark prefigure the best of 20th-century Scandinavian handmade furniture. In Sweden, although

A Swedish desk made by Georg Haupt, c1770, which shows the style and techniques he absorbed while training in Paris. The desk is in the Louis XVI style, and the quality of the marquetry is of Parisian standard. The piece is beautifully proportioned and the straight lines, the reticence of the mounts, the garlands and dependent lines of husks place it as Neoclassical.

English influence was not so great, a new elegant simplicity marks the Neoclassical cane furniture of the 1790s.

Russia and Poland

There is little indication of what Russian or Polish furniture was like before the 18th century. The early history of both countries is made up of civil strife and invasion and it is unlikely that anything other than a peasant tradition of very rudimentary furniture developed. It is known that in both countries textiles and wall painting played an important part in interior decoration and in Russia especially oriental fabrics influenced design. Surviving furniture from even the 18th and 19th centuries is less common than in Western Europe owing to the vicissitudes of Polish history and the appalling devastation suffered by Poland and Russia in World War II.

In the early 18th century Dutch and German Baroque exerted a strong influence but by the mid century inspiration derived mainly from the French Rococo. Polish Rococo approximated closely to its prototype whereas the Russian variety tended towards overstatement. The furniture of Rastrelli, the greatest of the designer-architects to work in Russia before the reign of Catherine the Great, exemplifies this tendency, particularly in the violence of the colors he employed. Furniture making in Russia and Poland resulted from a social structure unlike that obtaining in Western Europe.

A sofa designed by Count Bartolomeo Rastrelli, c1750. He was primarily an architect. The brilliant color and flamboyant carving mark out this piece as distinctively Russian.

POLAND

An armchair in cut steel made at Tula in the late 18th century. The back and side panels are decorated with copper. The piece shows the Russian use of ideas derived from the Roman Empire via Byzantium. The form is that of a Roman folding chair, which combined with the oriental lavishness and relative coarseness of execution mark this piece as decisively Russian.

The country estates of the aristocracy were, in many cases, enormous. They contained vast resources of manpower and of raw material. Although the courts at St Petersburg and Warsaw attracted foreign designers and cabinet-makers and large quantities of furniture were purchased directly from abroad, much furniture was made in the workshops of country estates. In the 18th century the furniture produced at Kolbuszova, one of the major Polish estates, was so well known and highly regarded that the name has come to be used as a general term for much fine Polish estate-produced furniture of the 18th and 19th centuries. Kolbuszova work often employed walnut veneers and stylized floral marquetry as did near-by estates. The standard of execution was high and an interesting compromise was reached between imported high fashion and indigenous peasant traditions. The comparable Russian synthesis was often less happy, particularly when the Russian element predominated; over-elaboration and coarse detail resulted.

Russian court-made furniture of the reign of Catherine II (1762–96) followed French models or, through the influence of Catherine's Scottish-born architect, Charles Cameron, the work of Robert Adam. Poland, too, in the latter part of the century, showed a strong Anglo-French influence, producing furniture of great delicacy, some of it made by craftsmen who had been imported from the Roentgen factory at Neuwied. Cut steel furniture was made at the Imperial small arms factory at Tula from the early 18th century and became fashionable under Catherine II. Most of it lacks the elegance of similar work from the Matthew Boulton factory in Birmingham, but, just as a provincialism in design in some Russian furniture was compensated for by the magnificence of the materials used—malachite table tops are an example—so at Tula an effect of almost barbaric splendor was produced by encrusting pieces with cut steel beads. Perhaps the most attractive of Tula's wares were those in which cut steel frames support a copper filigree.

A Russian secretaire made between 1810 and 1820. The finely figured karellian birch was very popular for Russian Neoclassical furniture. David Roentgen's influence can be seen in this piece, but lightness has been converted into heaviness and there is a provincial stolidity about it.

NORTH AMERICA

For much of its early history, America borrowed and adapted the shapes of English furniture. However, by the 18th century beautiful and original kinds of furniture were being developed. Regional centers produced their own specialities making use of differing materials.

The Dutch and Spanish inhabitants of New Amsterdam (now New York) and Florida left no furniture of certain American origin. Surviving examples of the earliest American furniture were produced by the English settlers of New England, at first mainly by the settlers of Massachusetts and Connecticut.

The forms of this furniture are in some ways reminiscent of an earlier period in English history and in others recall the contemporary furnishings of Puritan England. Necessity and Puritan ideology combined to produce a simple, dignified style. Ornament, when it occurs, tends to be crude and overstated. The style, known as American Jacobean, can be dated c1650–c1690.

The trestle table was produced in response to the need for furniture which could be easily dismantled to enable the main room of the house to serve a number of

Left: A gate-leg table, the base and legs too solid for the weight they have to bear. This example has a marbleized top.

Right: Two examples of trestle tables. The upper table could be easily stored and quickly assembled. The lower framed table has a bench attached.

purposes. Framed tables were also made, sometimes with detachable tops. Supports were usually either chamfered or turned. Both types of table obtain a certain elegance from their simplicity. The gate-leg table could also have this quality, but some examples show the unfortunate, and not infrequent result of attempting a style which the craftsman himself insufficiently understood. The base and legs are far too massive for the weight they have to bear and the outcome is a piece of furniture at once lumpy and depressing. The Cromwellian hybrid, the chair table, can be found at this period in America as in England, sometimes with a drawer under the seat.

Although benches and stools, often with splayed legs, were the most common form of seating, three types of chair were produced; the wainscot chair, with a paneled back, often heavily carved; and the Carver and Brewster chairs, named after two early colonists. These latter are armchairs in which all the principal members: arms, legs, stretchers and back supports are turned. The virtue of simplicity in design, particularly when craftsmanship and an awareness of tradition

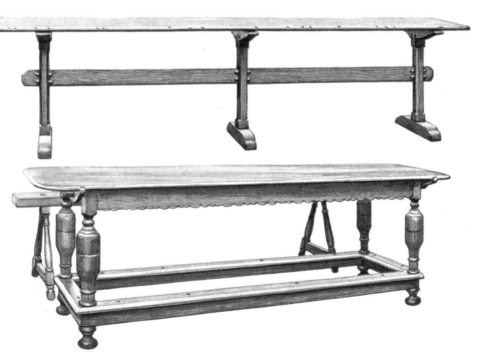

Top: An example of
the Brewster chair,
with its double rows of
spindles.
Below: A Carver chair.
The sensibly placed
handrests are the one
element of comfort at a
time when there were
no easychairs.

176

were in short supply, is exemplified by the difference between these two types of chair. The Carver normally has a single row of spindles forming the back, whereas the Brewster has a double row of spindles at the back, a double row at the front, below the seat, and often a row under each arm. The Carver's unpretentious design works. The Brewster resembles an unfinished cage.

In England the Restoration of the monarchy in 1660 ushered in a period of luxury and ostentation which did not start in America until the first use of fine veneers c1690. This was the beginning of the William and Mary period, a style which continued to be fashionable in America until the 1720s. In England the style had been superseded by both the Queen Anne and the early Georgian styles before the end of that decade.

Seat and case furniture developed more in the William and Mary period than at any earlier time. Cane was introduced as a seating material and the day bed with a woven cane base and a thin stuffed cushion acting as a mattress became fairly common; it was probably used for invalids, rather than, in the French style, as a lounging chair for the healthy. Upholstered easychairs appeared with wide, comfortably cushioned seats and turned stretchers. Slat-backed or ladder-backed chairs had been made in the Jacobean period but now became the standard chair in most American households. Slats were either bowed or straight. The tops of the back uprights were often finished with mushroom finials. Particular to America and used for all types of seat and table furniture were the bun foot and the paint brush foot, whose elegant outward pointing shape recalls that of the head of a paint brush pressed lightly against a hard surface. For fine furniture walnut and maple replaced oak as the most widely used carcase wood.

Three highly individual forms of case furniture were developed. By early in the 17th century chests had been found to be inadequate but it was only at the end of the century that the highboy, the lowboy and the *kas* came into popular use. The highboy was a chest-of-drawers on a stand not unlike contemporary European cabinets on stands except that the gilding and the vastly expensive European decoration of tortoiseshell, ivory and semi-precious stones was replaced by cheaper but very decorative burr wood veneers. Burr walnut and maple were popular. The lowboy was a truncated highboy, a single drawer or layer of drawers on a stand.

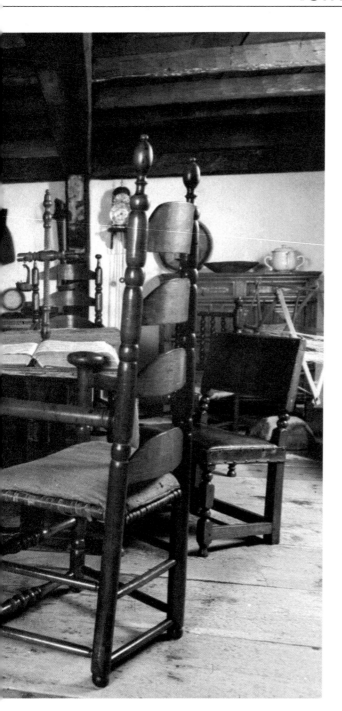

A room of 17th-century furniture, set out as it would have appeared originally, though more crowded. Many versions were made of the occasional table in the foreground: this one has a baluster-shaped column. The armchair in the foreground is grander than most. The shaping at the top of the ladder-back splats was, however, common, as were the turned finials at the top of the back members. Behind the armchair is a chair with a leather seat and back, of a kind taken from England. It is similar to the Spanish *sillón de fraileros*. On the left is an armchair, made entirely of turned work with a rush seat.

AMERICAN QUEEN ANNE

Left: A painted *kas* with bun feet, decorated with a popular design of fruit. It is made of oak. The painter has added an illusion of perspective to make the fruit stand out.

Opposite: Two American chairs.

Right: A straight-legged Massachusetts ladder-back chair, c1760–70. Made of mahogany, it is a development of earlier slatted country chairs, but the influence of Chippendale can be seen in the angling of the back leg, the fine proportions and the delicately pierced slats which form the back.

Far right: A Philadelphia tasselback chair, made of mahogany. Chippendale's influence is apparent in the claw and ball cabriole legs, and in the piercing of the back splat. The chair takes its name from the small carved tassel in the center of the splat.

The *kas* was the major contribution of the Dutch settlers to American furniture. It was produced in the early 18th-century, particularly in the area around New York. It was a large, simply constructed cupboard painted overall with bunches of flowers and fruit. It often had a projecting cornice top and small plain feet.

As urban American society became more sophisticated requiring furniture to carry out more precise and individual functions, it developed its own form of the secretary, the English drop-front desk. Many are very delicately inlaid and painted.

The English drop-leaf table was transplanted to America and gained butterfly-shaped hinged brackets which opened out to support the extended table top.

The Queen Anne period of American furniture occurred after the Queen's death and ran from c1720 to c1750 or 1760. The cabriole leg appears ubiquitously throughout the style except in one case, that of the Windsor chair. Although colonial furniture was often made for city people a folk element survived in it and c1720 Windsor chairs, a form of the English country chair with a round slatted back and arms and turned legs set at an oblique angle to the seat, became enormously popular in both simple and grand houses. They were produced in America in large numbers throughout the 18th century.

The writing arm Windsor chair was an American invention. Its right arm formed a desk top with a small drawer for sand and quills below; it also had a pull-out candle stand. This may be the first sign of the American fondness for improvisation and experiment in furniture so current in the 19th century.

Restrained curves are characteristic of nearly all the furniture of the period. Along with the cabriole leg, pad feet or three-toed feet were usual. The sofa replaced the daybed in popularity and normally had six legs.

AMERICAN QUEEN ANNE

Dining chairs gained a single curved vertical back splat in place of the horizontal splats of the ladder-back chair.

Ornament became more elegant. A finely carved fan shape decorated the fronts of lowboys and highboys. A delicately sculpted shell covered the knee of the cabriole leg. Boat-shaped handles replaced the tear-drop pulls of the William and Mary style. Japanning was carried out in Boston from the early 18th century. The quality of the work was less good than in Europe and in the course of time work has decayed badly. Enough

A room of American furniture from the middle of the 18th century. All the furniture has cabriole legs. The highboy on the right has pad feet, as does the chair on the extreme left. Highboys often had hanging decorations

similar to this one. The chair on the left follows a style well out of fashion in England. The circular table is a more sophisticated version of the occasional table. It is more elegant and well-proportioned.

remains for it to be apparent that when newly made it must have possessed a certain grace.

Regional variations were apparent early in American furniture making but so far as materials were concerned came to importance in the Queen Anne period. Although black walnut was used throughout the Eastern seaboard cherry was popular in New York and maple in New England and Philadelphia.

The Chippendale period in America (c1760–90) represents the culmination of colonial design. The cabriole leg gained the claw and ball foot. Shell or plant decoration on chair knees, shell tops to the pierced back splats of upright chairs and in Philadelphia, the insertion of a small tassel ornament in the center of the pierced splat (which accounts for the term "Philadelphia tassel-back") mark the maturity of American Rococo. The War of Independence of 1775–1783 made the importation of English furniture unpatriotic and impractical but did not prevent the use of Chippendale's *Gentleman and Cabinet-Maker's Directory* as the bible of the new style.

The term Rococo is only partially applicable to American furniture. In England, the lightness and frivolity of the true Rococo appears in the designs of Thomas Johnson and in some Chippendale mirror frames, but in American 18th-century furniture frivolity is completely lacking.

The greater proportion of furniture made in the second half of the 18th century was constructed from local woods of which tulipwood, maple and cherry were regularly used. Well-to-do merchants and farmers were catered for and country furniture in local woods with simplified decoration in the Chippendale manner seem to have been popular. However furniture in other styles continued to be made: the Pennsylvanian corner cupboard with a wave-curved broken pediment top can still be found.

By the mid-18th century Pennsylvanian German (misnamed Dutch) settlers had started to produce a rustic furniture of their own. Its two main additions to the American repertory were long rectangular dower chests with painted floral panels and borders and the *schrank*, a cupboard very similar to the Dutch *kas*.

For fine furniture mahogany was as fashionable in America as in England. It was used superbly. Regional variations of style became clearer since the basic material was constant. Philadelphia and Newport, Rhode

ROCOCO

Island were the biggest centers of furniture working. Philadelphia is famous for its highboys and for its chest-on-chests. The chest-on-chest often has small curved feet rather like the horse-hoof foot on Chinese tables. It carries pierced brass keyhole surrounds and boat handles on drawers and at the side of each chest section. Wave-curved broken pediments and open flame finials are common to chest-on-chests and highboys. At its best the Philadelphia highboy is a fine piece of 18th-century design. Newport also produced highboys but the Philadelphia version often has slightly shorter legs and carries a larger amount of carved decoration. This often includes swags of flowers or a shell carved in relief below the pediment and in the center of the skirt, tendrils on the knees and greater depth in the carving of the claws on the claw and ball feet.

Of named Philadelphia craftsmen William Savery made lowboys and chairs in a transitional style between Queen Anne and Chippendale Rococo. His work lacks the elaboration of the great highboys. Benjamin Randolph produced chairs in a full Rococo style. The Englishman Thomas Affleck was especially fond of the straight "Marlboro" leg and his chairs have a powerful, monumental quality. A fourth Pennsylvania cabinet maker, Jonathan Gostelowe is known for his sweep front chests-of-drawers.

The most famous Newport furniture makers were of the two related families of Goddard and Townsend, of which some 20 members were workers in the furniture trade. A number of them were loyalists as was Affleck, but whereas Affleck throve after the war John Goddard's business was ruined by the war and he died in debt. John Townsend managed to make the necessary political transition, abandoned the Rococo for the Federal mode and continued to make a living.

Perhaps the most attractive pieces of furniture associated with the two families are the block-front secretaries, the drop-front desks and chest-on-chests of Newport. The name "block-front" refers to the articulation of the front of the piece in which two vertical rectangles stand proud of the main body flanking a sunken rectangle. The top and bottom of each rectangle is often completed with a fan or shell shape. Similar pieces without the fan were made in Massachusetts and New York. Benjamin Frothingham of Massachusetts used this simplified pattern of blocking

A Salem secretary, made by Nehemiah Adams between 1780 and 1805. This example of Salem cabinet-making is veneered in mahogany. It was discovered in Capetown. North America had considerable overseas trade in fine furniture in the late 18th century.

on the lower section of chest-on-chests and secretaries.

Although the Federal period (1790–1830) continues into the 19th century it contains two essentially 18th-century developments: the influence of the Neoclassicism of Robert Adam through the designs of Hepplewhite and Sheraton; and that of French furni-

FEDERAL STATE

ture of the last years of the Ancien Régime and of the Directory.

French encouragement to the colonies in the War of Independence led to a North American interest in French fashions. The republican associations of the Directory may also have made an appeal. For whatever reason the saber legs of the Directory (and of the English Regency) and the straight legs of Hepplewhite and Sheraton replaced the cabriole leg. Paint or satinwood veneers and string banding replaced carved mahogany for seat, table and case furniture although country districts continued to use their native woods without veneer. Hepplewhite wheel-backed chairs with carved and painted Prince of Wales feathers appeared.

Philadelphia continued as a center of furniture production but Boston, and above all, Salem and New York developed their own important industries too. Each city exported furniture. Salem sold furniture not only in other states but in South Africa and South America as well. Its best known creation was the Salem secretary, an attractive knee-hole drop-front writing desk with a break-front upper section (where the central section projects) which usually took the form of a glass fronted bookcase. The most famous name in Salem's furniture industry was Samuel McIntyre who appears to have been more important as a carver of furniture decoration than as a joiner or cabinet maker. In Boston an English immigrant, John Seymour, made furniture with a mixture of fine veneers and painted decoration which became a feature of the city's style. His firm also produced well-constructed examples of the newly fashionable lady's tambour desk, a form of desk that was drum shaped, and rested on short legs.

In the Federal period New York's most distinguished furniture maker was Duncan Phyfe. Though his later work is in the Empire Style, at the beginning of the 19th century he was working in Hepplewhite, Sheraton and Directory styles, using, in the main, mahogany. It is in his continued use of this wood (although he also employed the more fashionable satinwood) that one of his elements of originality lay. He took the motifs of Neoclassicism and gave them weight and solidity from the weight and solidity of the materials he employed. Compared with genuine Sheraton or Directory furniture Phyfe's sometimes lacks delicacy but he could convey dignity very well. Of comparable ability was the French

Right: A New York mahogany scroll-backed chair with a lyre bannister of c1810–1820. The design is similar to one of Duncan Phyfe's, except that in his design the front legs end in hairy paw feet. The design is clearly based on Directoire or English Regency chairs, themselves based on the Ancient Greek *klismos*.

Far right: A New England variant of a Hepplewhite design, probably made c1795. Mahogany shield-back chairs like this one were made in many New England areas, but especially fine examples carved with great skill are often associated with the name of Samuel McIntire of Salem. The carving in the shield back is more florid than in most examples.

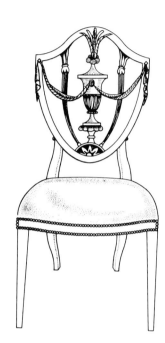

immigrant Charles Honoré Lannuier.

Baltimore was strongly influenced by French Neo-classical forms in furniture but it was the Neoclassicism of Carlin and Weisweiler rather than of the Directory. Where Carlin might have used Sèvres plaques in his work Baltimore craftsmen employed panels of *verre eglomisé* (gilded and colored glass) depicting allegorical figures.

The types of furniture popular in the Federal period differed considerably from those popular in the Rococo period. The highboy and lowboy were regarded as old-fashioned. Sofas became more common. The specifically American Martha Washington armchair appeared with its tall thin back and open arms. Pembroke tables took the place of tea-tables and the sideboard and extending dining tables were introduced into the dining room.

COLONIAL FURNITURE

Colonial residents took full advantage of the exotic materials that became available to them. Quite ordinary furniture was reproduced in ivory or silver; tortoise-shell, mother-of-pearl and ivory were commonly used for veneers. Bamboo and cane were found appropriate for every-day living.

India and South East Asia

Europeans in the East sought a mixture of the familiar and the exotic in their furniture. In the late 17th century the Dutch asked the Chinese to make and decorate European style dinner services; the Indian and Ceylonese produced European cupboards and chairs for the Portuguese, the Dutch and the English, sometimes in exotic materials and sometimes with Eastern decoration. European demands varied according to their relationship with the colonial country. In China (except in the tiny enclaves of Hong Kong and Macao), Europeans were just traders ordering goods like other traders. In India, Ceylon and the East Indies they were more or less permanent residents. Much of the furniture produced for the Portuguese in Goa, for the British throughout India and for the Dutch in the East Indies, therefore, is not technically export work. It is colonial work. Settlers wanted furniture to serve the function it had served in England, Portugal or Holland but they were pleased to have it made in the exotic woods, ivory or metals of the countries in which they found themselves.

In the 17th century Goa became one of the world's richest towns as its position as middleman between the Far East and Europe was exploited. The Portuguese spent considerable amounts of money on their furniture and a new style, the Goan Portuguese, was born. The forms of European tables, cupboards and chairs

Two examples of colonial furniture. On the left is an early 18th-century revolving chair, made in India. It shows a mixture of European form and local technique. On the right is a Dutch burgomaster chair, made in the East Indies. In style it dates from the late 17th and early 18th centuries.

were usually retained by native craftsmen but the elaborate inlays of rosewood or ebony and ivory or bone set into a teak base used the motifs of Indian art. The earliest pieces, dating from the 17th century, often carry a leaf-scroll pattern which was replaced, in the 18th century, by an intricate series of circles. Legs were frequently carved in the round as human figures, mermaids or vegetation. In Ceylon no comparable style developed but the Portuguese commissioned ivory boxes and chests carved with pictures of themselves in their new surroundings or taking part in elephant rides

An Indian copy, in ivory, of a late 18th-century design. Around the seat the maker has faithfully copied, still in ivory, the nail heads which in a conventional piece of furniture would secure the seat upholstery. The small sunflower motif is typical of the work of Robert Adam, on whose work this chair is based. The little claw and ball feet at the front of the chair are unusual in a piece of this period. Chairs like this were commissioned by members of the East India Company.

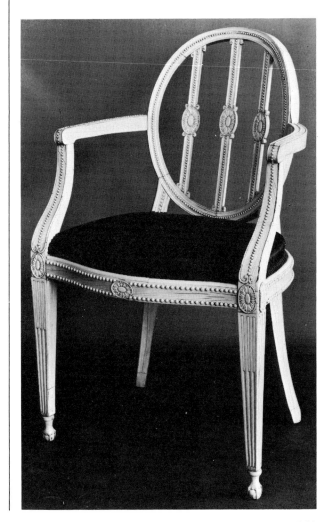

or tiger hunts.

Ivory was enormously popular with the Europeans in India, partly for its value, partly because it withstood the climate and insects better than wood. The Dutch settlements in India and the East Indies produced a number of burgomaster chairs made in ivory and for the English in the late 18th century Indian carvers made delightful ivory copies of Adam and Hepplewhite chairs.

Chairs in bamboo and cane were particularly popular with the British in India and the Dutch in the East Indies. Its lightness, coolness and resistance to insects made it ideal compared to upholstered furniture.

Central and South America

The Spanish and Portuguese colonies of South America grew out of different circumstances and their furniture developed in different ways. In Mexico in 1519 and Peru in 1534, the Spaniards smashed two civilizations; the forms that developed were influenced partly by native arts and partly by the wealth of the conquered countries. In Brazil during the 16th and 17th centuries the Portuguese slowly colonized a sparsely and primitively populated region, which was not very valuable except for dye-woods. In the course of the 17th century some Dutch merchants landed and were absorbed into the society. It was only with the discovery of gold in Brazil in the late 17th century and of diamonds in 1728 that a wealthy Brazilian society developed and spectacular furniture was made.

The riches of Spanish America produced a demand for luxury goods very early. In Bogota c1650 Miguel de Acuña was making ebony cabinets veneered with engraved ivory and tortoiseshell. At the same time a fashion had been imported into Lima from the Philippines; large pieces of furniture were veneered with sections of mother-of-pearl bound together with thin frames of silver or ivory. Chairs at the Vice-regal court in Lima and in the grander homes of the city were covered with sheets of repoussé silver. Amongst the wealthy in Lima silver and mother-of-pearl were enormously popular for furniture.

During the 17th century curves became more pronounced with the development of Spanish Baroque architecture. In the 18th century the heaviness of Baroque work persisted both in Mexico and Peru, although the efforts of one 18th-century Viceroy, Don

A Peruvian colonial sofa, reflecting the local version of Rococo. Spanish influence of the 18th century is clear from the shape and length of the piece. The influence of English chair design on this piece's Spanish prototypes is evident in the repeated chair back splats. The carved sections are less clear-cut than in equivalent Spanish work, and hard edges are avoided.

Manuel Afat, to introduce a lighter Rococo style proved partly successful.

Brazil's early history as a furniture-producing country has none of the glitter of Peru or Mexico. During the 17th and early 18th centuries the combined Portuguese and Dutch influence seems to have been responsible for the use of wave-moldings. The close-grained Brazilian hardwoods were ideal for the intricate turned work which was so popular in Portugal and in Brazil the exotic form of the Portuguese bed was loaded with decorative work of this kind.

Even at the end of the 18th century the Portuguese Baroque with its massive flowing forms was the usual furniture style in Brazil. In 1808 members of the Portuguese court arrived, fleeing from the armies of Napoleon. They brought with them the Neoclassicism of contemporary Europe which was adapted to the by now sumptuous tastes of a colony which had grown rich on diamonds. Veneers which in Europe were of wood were replaced by mother-of-pearl and ivory.

191

19th CENTURY

Industrialization led to the first mass-production of furniture. It also created a nostalgia for the past. This led to a chaotic choice of styles from previous eras, and later in the century to a taste for country furniture.

During the 19th and 20th centuries a new society was forced into shape by political and economic changes in a Europe still partly feudal. Increasingly rapid communications meant that differences of style between country and country, not least in superficial matters, tended to disappear. The population was increasing. By the 1840s there was an enormous demand for manufactured goods; mechanization made their production possible, but also ensured a large degree of stereotyping across the continent.

In England, France and Germany a vast, rich, new middle class came into being, and it was their taste that was reflected in most of the furniture that was produced. In the 1850s and 1860s this taste ran to elaboration. To put it plainly, they wanted their money's worth and they wanted it to be seen that they had money. Rich upholstery and ostentatious decoration became the necessary expressions of material success. In due course, a reaction to this ostentation took place. Led by John Ruskin and the Arts and Crafts movement of William Morris in England, men of taste urged a return to simplicity and to ideals of the nobility of craftsmanship and labor. These values were ascribed to a hypothetical Medieval man, who would probably have been surprised by them. Though sentimental in outlook, the movement was influential in the decorative arts and led to the formation of small workshops of craftsmen who made furniture very different from that produced in great quantities by the factories. In this way the two modes of furniture-making which continue in all industrialized countries in the 20th century were established. The tradition of the small craftsman producing individual items of furniture, usually for rich patrons, lies side by side with the mass production of the factory.

1800–1830 In the opening years of the 19th century Europe was dominated by one political reality. For the first time since the fall of Rome, one man—Napoleon—effectively ruled the whole of the continent. Not only did Napoleon rule, he placed his family on the thrones

The cradle of the King of Rome. This version was made in 1811 by Jacob-Desmalter and Thomire, who produced the gilt bronze mounts. It is a simplified version, made for use in the Palace of the Tuileries, of the cradle made in the same year by Odiot and Thomire, in silver gilt and lapis lazuli. On this version an Imperial eagle with a crown of stars originally surmounted the canopy. The present figure was substituted after the Restoration of the Bourbons in 1814. The plaques on the cradle represent Napoleon's hopes for his son. On one side the Seine and the arms of Paris are represented, on the other the Tiber and the arms of Rome: the double Empire Napoleon wished to leave him. Figures of peace and justice are at the head and foot. There is no finer example of French First Empire furniture.

of Europe; these included Holland, Spain, Westphalia and the Italian states (Rome and the Western littoral becoming part of France itself). In the 18th century the style of the French court was the origin of the styles adopted in most European courts. Under Napoleon the style employed in Paris was used by his relatives with few regional variations. Subject and allied monarchs — Russian and Austrian — followed suit.

The Empire style was designed specifically to suggest Antique grandeur. The intention was to surround the Emperor and his regime with the panoply appropriate to an absolute monarch; by drawing on the past for analogies of power it also gave his rule a spurious legitimacy. In this lies the great weakness in the Empire style, a weakness that reflects a political mistake. In a new position which he had created, he needed a new society and a new style. Instead he replaced the top members of the hierarchy of the old society with his own nominees. In furnishing, the architects Percier and Fontaine provided him with a flattering but empty rhetoric.

The Empire style was at its best before the Empire itself existed. Napoleon's expedition to Egypt, his victory over the Mamelukes at the Battle of the Pyramids in 1798 and the presence of scholars in Napoleon's entourage recording the country's monuments made Egyptian motifs especially popular despite the fact that the expedition was ultimately a failure. These motifs were married with the Classical motifs inherited from Louis XVI furniture and with symbols or reminders of military prowess. When Mme Bonaparte (later the Empress Josephine) engaged the architects Percier and Fontaine to decorate and furnish the Château of Malmaison in 1799, pieces of furniture embodying these motifs still served the accepted, ordinary function of furniture. Later pieces became increasingly grandiose as the process of the near deification of Napoleon advanced.

The Empire lasted from 1804 to 1814. Napoleon was concerned to establish his credibility as Emperor with other European monarchs, not only for his own lifetime by military success but also for the dynasty he hoped to found. Naturally this was a political ambition that could only be achieved politically, but Napoleon understood the importance of staging. The Empire style as created for him by Percier and Fontaine was the furnishing of an enormous stage set.

It was partly the speed with which Napoleon wanted the set mounted that accounts for the great use made of draperies in the period. Curtains were hung on walls as well as windows. Rooms became luxurious versions of military tents with curtains looped back to reveal mirrors extending the vistas of the room. Magnificence combined with comfort and a constant reiteration of past authority through the use of emblems of antiquity dominated decor.

A consideration of even one room of the period includes a remarkable number of such emblems and motifs. In 1810 a bedroom was decorated for the

Furniture reflects the shapes of the Classical revival in architecture; churches resemble Antique temples. Large mirrors on stands are a new form; also portable dressing-table swivel mirrors.

Decorations, the sphinx and winged lion (Egyptian) and the caryatid (Classical).

Named Empire style in France, Regency in England, Neoclassical furniture reflected the contemporary preoccupation with the Classical past of Greece and Rome. Napoleon's victory in Egypt in 1798 led to a fashion for Egyptian decorations. English styles derive from France. Dark woods, mahogany and rosewood are typical of the period. Brass was used for inlay, handles, casters and feet to provide a contrast. Satinwood and gilded bronze were also popular.

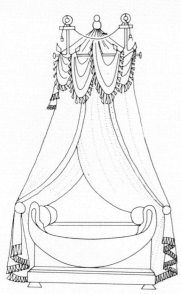

A boat-shaped bed. The long necked swan, often used on Empire decoration, the Empress Josephine's favourite bird.

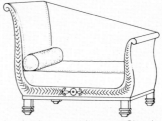

A day-bed, or *méridienne*; a Classical shape. Bolsters were common.

Motifs in gilded bronze decorated furniture. Stars, palmettes, medallions, Imperial eagle and the Napoleonic bee were all typically French. Oval patera were popular in England, especially on veneered furniture.

Saber legs were typical of Regency chairs.

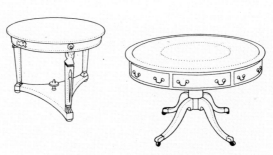

Tables: usually round. In England, the legs centrally placed, in France, fixed at the edges.

Empress Josephine at Malmaison. It is in the form of a Classical military tent with great swathes of red cloths supported on gilded wooden poles. The bed reflects the shape of a tent and is surmounted by the Imperial eagle. The inner curtains of the bed are embroidered with Napoleon's own emblem, the bee. The curtains at the foot of the bed are supported on a framework composed of gilded poles, each tipped with a pine cone; thyrsi, the fruition giving staves of the followers of Dionysus. The bed foot is decorated with gilded cornucopiae, again symbols of fruitfulness. Clearly it was hoped that placed here they might prove good auguries for the conception of an heir by the Emperor and Empress. Thyrsian patterns recur on the carpet. An *athénienne* (washstand) continues the Classical mode. Its three legs, each with an animal's foot and knee, are topped by a gilded sphinx, recalling Napoleon's Egyptian connection. A *guéridon* (a circular table on a plinth and three legs) has winged lions as supports recalling the fabulous beasts of Egyptian and Classical mythology. Gilding and brilliant colors are in evidence throughout. Perhaps because it was made for a woman of taste the furniture here is more delicate than would usually be expected from the term "Empire". Much of the furniture made this late is unnecessarily monumental; design became so subordinated to expressing the Imperial message that furniture, which by its nature is not a suitable medium for propaganda, became rather dull and overemphatic with the constant repetition of the same motifs.

The standard of craftsmanship in France during the Empire was high, the most important group of craftsmen being probably the family Jacob. Georges Jacob had been a *menuisier* of great distinction under Louis XVI and continued to produce superb work in the Directory and Empire styles. His two sons took over from their father using, for their workshop stamp, the name "Jacob Frères". When one of the brothers died the firm continued under the name "Jacob-Desmalter".

Georges Jacob had begun his career as a *menuisier*, a maker of seat furniture. After the destruction of the guilds during the French Revolution the firm took over a wide range of furniture making and amongst its most outstanding commissions were jewel cabinets for the Empresses Josephine and Marie Louise, and the Louvre version of the cradle of the King of Rome, Napoleon's only legitimate son. Mahogany was much employed;

Top: The fashion for indoor plants grew in the Regency period. This plant stand is dated 1810, and resembles a Classical garden temple.

Below: A circular mirror, a distinctively Regency type.

so too were superbly produced gilt bronze mounts. Thomire, perhaps the finest French mount maker, designed the mounts for the Louvre cradle. For the version now in Vienna he cast his work in silver and gilded it. Indeed the Vienna cradle, designed by Odiot and made by Thomire, is magnificent goldsmith's rather than furniture maker's work. (The two versions of this cradle were made for different palaces.)

Where the Napoleonic writ ran, in Germany, Italy and Spain, the same style was adopted. David Roentgen's furniture for the palaces in Berlin produced during Napoleon's reign is pure Empire. The same motifs and forms as were used in Paris were repeated in what were now virtually French territories. In Germany the style lasted only as long as the Empire itself. In Italy it was continued for palace furniture, perhaps because so many states of Italy had become for a while the property of individual members of the Bonaparte family. All five of Napoleon's brothers and sisters were rulers of various parts of the peninsula at one time or another, as was his stepson. The interior of their palaces they transformed into French palaces with French furniture. Local carpenters copied French models. When the former occupants of the palaces were restored to their positions the contents were so much more attractive than they had been previously that they were retained and their style continued to be emulated.

In Holland the Empire style, imported by Napoleon's brother Louis, continued after 1814. The same occurred in Spain, where the "Fernandino" style, a sumptuous and at times vulgarized version of Empire, lasted for perhaps 15 years after Joseph Bonaparte had been driven from the Spanish throne. In Russia French Empire gave way to English influence more or less as the Czar Alexander I moved from a besotted admiration for the Emperor to alliance against him.

England was the only major European country that was not at any time conquered by or allied to Napoleon. Nevertheless, French taste had influenced English palace furniture from the time of Charles II and at the end of the 18th century the Prince of Wales, later Regent and then George IV, was a great admirer of the decorative arts of France. At Carlton House, his London home when Prince of Wales, he formed an enormous and very costly collection of furniture and pictures. His architect, Henry Holland, designed ceremonial furniture which drew strongly on Roman forms distilled through the work of Percier and Fontaine and which would have looked as appropriate in Paris, Vienna or St Petersburg as it did in London. However the development of English furniture and fine art has rarely been straightforward. In Carlton House the style of the last three Louis and of the Empire were brought together but there were also rooms decorated in the Gothic taste and furniture which strictly followed Classical models. Also, the Prince early showed the interest in Indian and Chinese curiosities which was to result in the fantasy palace of the Brighton Pavilion.

The Classicism of the Regency, which for furniture may be regarded as 1795 to 1830, (the actual years of Regency were 1810–20) was stricter than that of Robert Adam. Its early emergence can be seen in the pier tables supplied to Harewood House by Thomas Chippendale the Younger in 1795. Their garlanded monopodia have a remarkably antiquarian air. Correctness seems of more consequence than grace. The correctness continues in the book *Household furniture and Interior Decoration* produced for Thomas Hope in 1807 as a record of the furnishing of his London home. The surviving furniture from this house indicates an obsession with Classical shapes and motifs, including a large admixture of the Egyptian which had become popular in England at the same time as in France and for a similar reason. As France celebrated Napoleon's victory over the Mamelukes at the Battle of the Pyramids, England celebrated Nelson's destruction of Napoleon's fleet at the Battle of the Nile.

Sheraton's *Cabinet Dictionary* of 1803, and his *Cabinet-maker, Upholsterer and General Artists' Encyclopaedia* of 1804–06 drew together the main elements of English Regency style and, probably, introduced a few of them, including the scroll-ended Grecian couch and the use of animal heads on chair arms.

Although uprights formed the backs of chairs in the early years of the Regency period, by 1805 a new form based on the Greek *klismos* had appeared in which a horizontal curved band of wood supported the small of the back. Legs from being straight were turned outwards towards the foot, or, more commonly, (and more attractively), the back legs were curved backwards, the front legs forward in the distinctive Regency saber shape. After the Battle of Trafalgar in 1805, chairs with backs composed of two or more horizontal rails fixed

Right: An English Regency chair, of the very early 19th century. The decoration of the front legs is not unusual for this period: the striped apron and the tridents set into the uprights and the top rail are. With a turned rope motif replacing the center of the top rail, this chair would be a "Trafalgar" chair.

Above right: An armchair by Thomas Hope, one of a set of four designed for his own house in London between 1800 and 1807. The pedantry of his approach is illustrated by his description of this chair, relating the derivation of each motif. All the motifs are Egyptian. Earlier designs combined Egyptian, Greek and Roman elements with a fine disregard for propriety. The result here is "correct", but perhaps a little absurd.

on upright side supports often had the center of the top rail carved in a rope design, supposedly as a reference to the sea and the victory. Whilst this cannot be verified with certainty, it is true that as Nelson's list of victories grew motifs based on the sea increased in popularity and their popularity continued for some years after his death at Trafalgar.

George Smith's *Collection of Designs for Household Furniture and Interior Decoration* of 1808 brought to the middle classes the fashions created by the Prince of Wales and aristocratic patronage. Some of the designs shown are even more extreme and odd than those in Sheraton's *Encyclopaedia*—for example, ornament in the shape of crocodiles—but in general a high level of elegance was maintained. By the second decade of the 19th century decoration was becoming more florid. Brass patterns cut into complex patterns were combined with rosewood and zebrawood to form cabinet fronts and table pedestals. The method of cutting was similar to that employed by Boulle for Louis XIV and was generally called "Buhl work". In general it is the simpler furniture of the Regency, particularly its lovely

The dining room from Erddig Park, Wales. In the Regency period the British dining room no longer contained the great, often fixed, sideboards of Chippendale and the fixed, shaped side-tables of Adam. Lighter, movable sideboards were fashionable. The tables and chairs were supplied by the firm of Gillow of Lancaster in 1827. The room is typical of late Regency style.

chairs, sofas and low tables made for the middle classes or for the private apartments of the aristocracy, which shows the best design of the period.

The everyday furniture of the Regency was the heir of English Neoclassical furniture. This Neoclassical style began the anglomania of the 1780s in France and Germany and continued to influence German and Scandinavian non-state furniture for the first 30 years of the 19th century. In the 1780s the *Journal des Luxus und der Moden* in Germany was designed specifically to spread English fashions in furnishings. Its editor, F. J. J. Bertiuch, rhapsodized over the way in which the English, by tastefully marrying their study of Classical example to modern technology, had become the first to make radical improvements in their furniture, making it both more beautiful and more practical.

The lesson learnt from this produced, by 1815, the Biedermeier style in Germany. It is functional and spare. Chair legs are either straight or of a delicate saber style. Sofas tend to be rather square, but could be curved and were sometimes supplied with a round table. Mahogany was the most popular wood. From paintings of the period it can be seen that rooms were sparsely furnished, but they give an impression of delicately modulated space lacking in the more ornate and assertive salons of the Empire. In Berlin Friedrich Schinkel produced a style of his own for the furnishing of the palace at Charlottenburg. His work combines the elegance of Biedermeier with added decorative elements: motifs of sculpted ribbons or volutes at the end of a bed, drawn from the motifs of the 18th century.

In the United States the Federal style continued in use until the second decade of the 19th century. Then two New York desigers, Charles-Honoré Lannuier and Duncan Phyfe, introduced the heavier, more ornate manner of the Empire. Perhaps because he was a Frenchman and to some extent had direct experience of the Empire style Lannuier's furniture more closely resembles its European prototypes. Indeed he imported bronze mounts for his work from France. Phyfe had a more individual approach. He combined Empire modes with those of Regency England and produced a style that was a hybrid but a personal and unusually elegant hybrid. The quality of the workmanship of this craftsman was high. Furniture in the USA became more massive as the 1820s passed and as Empire ideas were absorbed, but a court and aristocracy were lacking so

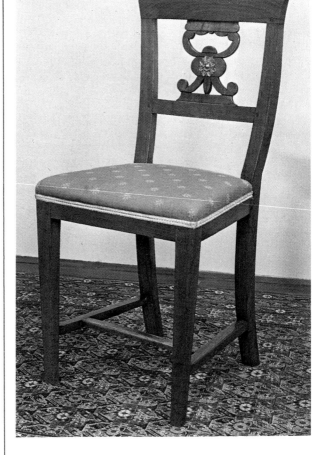

One of a pair of chairs in the Biedermeier style, of fruitwood with stamped brass mounts. Biedermeier furniture was made with almost aesthetic simplicity, and a concern for truth to materials. There is no attempt to hide the joints, and the screws are countersunk and covered over with visible wooden plugs.

no equivalent of the very grandest furniture of Europe was produced.

1830–1870   The period from the 1830s to the 1870s was one of transition, which led to some peculiar styles in furniture. Enormous economic, social and technological changes were taking place in Europe and America. Their effect on furniture was to produce pieces which used the most modern technical virtuosity in order to reproduce and elaborate a variety of styles dredged up from the past. These seem to have little relevance to the 19th century. Manufacturing tycoons, be they in Manchester, Lyons or Pittsburgh used the most modern machinery in their plants. However, they felt in using it that they were rivaling the work of handcarvers. They also considered that furniture should have reassuring historical associations: "improved" Rococo, Gothic, Louis XIV or Elizabethan, perhaps, or even a bit of all of them.

The development of the factory system is often blamed for the debasement of taste in furniture of this period. That is blaming the tool for the job. Machinery was misused, made to do jobs for which it was inappropriate. This may have been the result of an inability on the part of designer and public to conceive of a new style to meet new requirements. Alternatively, it may have been that the buying public felt a need to surround themselves with objects from a mocked-up past to give their homes an air of stability in the middle of the enormous flux of mid-19th-century life. It was these factors which led to the bad design of so much furniture at the time.

Technical innovations and the love of innovation for its own sake were also responsible for some ugly design. In London in 1828 Samuel Spratt patented wire springs for mattresses. By 1833 in his *Encyclopaedia of Cottage, Farm and Villa Architecture and Furniture* J. C Loudon refers as a matter of course to spring upholstery and by the 1840s, in one writer's phrase, furniture had become "marshmallows on legs".

Pressed paper, known erroneously as "papier-mâché", had been patented in England in 1772, but only began widely to replace wood in furniture making with the firm of Jennens and Bettridge in the 1830s. Although many of the firm's small articles are now greatly admired, (particularly those produced early in their output), the only admiration likely to be given to their pressed and japanned bed head-boards and chair backs, decorated with mother-of-pearl, would be for the ingenuity which went into employing so inappropriate a material when wood and metal were available.

Although "papier-mâché" lent itself to being pressed into unusual and exotic shapes, wood did not until John Henry Belter in New York invented lamination. By steam-heating laminated rosewood in molds he was able to produce pressed versions of Louis XV furnishings. He applied the same technique, but more rarely, to oak and to ebonized wood. In the 1850s and 1860s he sometimes added carved sections in solid wood to his pieces. He specialized particularly in ex-

Even in France Neo-Gothic furniture was made.

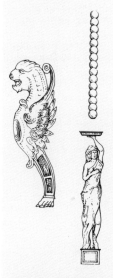

Renaissance and 17th-century motifs rioted over furniture. Often crude and over-emphatic.

By the mid-19th century, style had been replaced by styles. A confused mixture of elements were drawn from different historical periods. Materials were almost as various. Papier mâché and cast iron, besides wood, became important materials for furniture. Upholstery was much used for seat furniture. Heavy curtains and tablecloths added to the stuffiness of drawing and dining rooms. Elegance gave way to clutter, with the taste for what-nots, occasional tables and ornaments.

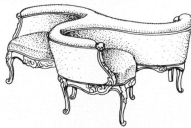

Mid century English work: Rococo applied to new materials like *papier-mâché*.

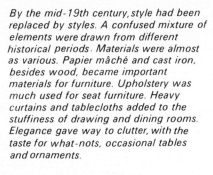

Bavaria in the 1870s over-used Rococo motifs.

French work of the 1850s used Rococo style for new sorts of furniture like this "indiscret".

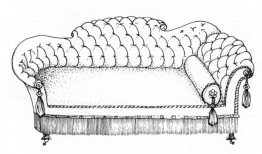

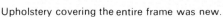

Rocking chairs were popular, of wood or metal.

Upholstery covering the entire frame was new.

tremely complex Rococo designs but later in his career also adopted Renaissance ornament. The standard of skill was high, of design, questionable, and according to the viewer's taste.

Metals, particularly iron, were much employed in the mid-Victorian period. Metal beds had been made as early as the 17th century but late 18th-century and early 19th-century studies of hygiene suggested that metal would be more sanitary than wood as a material for construction and tubular frames were patented in 1812. By the 1840s the Victorian iron bedstead with its brass knobs was common in England. It was, however, the malleability of iron which was found intriguing in the mid-19th century, particularly in the United States, France and England. During the 1860s and 1870s furniture for gardens and summerhouses became enormously popular; it included cast iron chairs, benches and tables, many shaped like rough-hewn logs or trellises of branches and flowers. One of the more elegant products of the period was the English cast iron garden chair with a seat made of springy flat metal rods which met in the center of the seat to form a cushion.

After the upholstery spring, the second invention most influential in aiding the degeneration of furniture design was T. B. Jordan's wood-carving machine of 1845. Several pieces of identical decoration could now be cut out at the same time. Since intricate carving was in vogue, tortured pieces of wood disguised as furniture flooded Europe and America. As societies in the British colonies of Canada, Australia and New Zealand developed they also received the blessing of such pieces from the mother country or from the United States. Fortunately, however, their technology was insufficient for them to copy complicated forms and they continued to produce furniture which derived directly from the folk idioms of an earlier period.

Folk furnishings continued to be produced throughout Europe and America until late into the 19th century. In England, France and Germany local joiners used the idioms of plain furniture of the 17th and 18th centuries to serve both their own needs and those of their immediate neighbourhood. In England, where industrialization had occurred more rapidly than elsewhere, a whole range of furniture makers existed. At one end were village carpenters and the specialized furniture makers of an area. Their work would have been known and accepted in lower- and middle-class

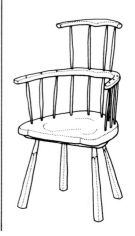

Three variations of the Windsor chair, examples of English rustic furniture.

A Windsor chair, probably the quintessential English country chair. It was developed in the second half of the 18th century. This example is made of ash with an elm seat and turned leg and arm supports. Beech was the material used most often for Windsor chairs.

homes throughout the country and even abroad (the makers of Windsor chairs at High Wycombe are the best known example). In the middle of the spectrum were the sophisticated provincial makers at York, Bristol, Leeds, Cambridge and Wakefield who supplied the well-to-do of the region: one particularly well-known company was that of Gillow at Lancaster, to which Hepplewhite had been apprenticed; it supplied furniture to many of the aristocratic houses of Northern England and Scotland. At the top end of the market were the major London firms such as Holland and Crace.

The folk tradition in the United States continued to develop mainly owing to the activities of isolated groups like the Shakers.

The Shakers were ascetics. Mother Ann Lee, their first great leader in the New World, specifically warned against the worldliness of owning "costly and extrava-

An early 19th-century Shaker dining chair, showing the extreme simplicity of the sect's furniture. The rush seat and turned members are completely unadorned. The only ornamental feature is the gentle curve which tops the back splat.

gant furniture." The Shakers' ideas about design and construction considerably predate those of the Bauhaus and although they spring from very different premises are all but indistinguishable from them. Both eschew ornament and stress functionalism. Both regard the house and its contents as a single working entity. The 20th-century's concern for saving space was shared by the Shakers: as in the early colonial period dining tables were often supplied with detachable tops but storage problems were dealt with in a novel way. Built-in cupboards had been common in grand houses from the Renaissance. The Shakers built storage units as part of the fabric of their houses. To solve the problem of storing chairs and small pieces of furniture the Shaker equivalent of stacking furniture was the provision of a pegged board running at head height around a room on which pieces of furniture not in use could be hung.

SHAKER FURNITURE

In Shaker furniture simple elegant shapes were combined to make a utilitarian whole. Materials were respected and craftsmanship was of a high order. Chairs and tables could be spare and delicate, since their strength lay in sound construction. The only decoration used was color. Paints and stains of shades of the primary colors and of green were applied to give a cheerful appearance to the interior of a Shaker house.

In the religio-social basis of their designs the Shakers differed profoundly from other producers of "simple" furniture such as the early American colonists, or the designers of Utility furniture in the United Kingdom during World War II. The simplicity of early colonial furniture, though it may have been related to Puritanism, was mainly the result of lack of skill. Utility furniture was the result of having to pare to the most basic level everything which did not contribute to the war effort in order to survive. In Shaker furniture ideology and skill marry in simple yet satisfying work.

The commercial exploitation of the Neo-Rococo had begun in England (in the 1840s), and France (c1835), and had rapidly spread throughout Europe, even to Scandinavia, which had been little influenced by the original Rococo. Commercial Neo-Gothic began in England and caught the imagination of people elsewhere, particularly in Germany and the Low Countries. The naturalistic style appeared almost everywhere in the mid-19th century. To some extent this was an original idea, fostered initially by wood carvers who saw elaborate carvings of fruit, flowers and figures as one area where they could beat the machines but by the 1850s machine carving had caught up, at least superficially.

The series of Great Exhibitions, beginning with the Crystal Palace Exhibition of 1851 in London, encouraged both hand-carvers and machinists to attempt work on a massive scale and, since intricacy was admired, to cover their works with minute detail. Every surface had to be busy. In reaction to this work William Morris created the setting for the Arts and Crafts Movement in England. In the 1830s the architect A. W. Pugin had tried to simplify design by returning to a "correct" instead of an "improved" Gothic style but his efforts met with little response at the time. Morris continued Pugin's work but although the attempt was laudable it was not altogether successful. Philip Webb and J. P. Seddon designed furniture for Morris, some of which was excellent but two things prevented it fulfilling the function for which Morris had set up his firm in 1861. First, the simple furniture, which revealed the best design, did not make much appeal to the rich and, being hand-made, was far too expensive for the poor. Second, in order to compete with commercial design the firm began to produce elaborate display pieces to show at the Exhibitions. These were of superior quality to much else that went into the Exhibitions but since they were usually large pieces, painted with Medieval decorations and carved with Medieval motifs they, just as much as Neo-Rococo furniture, were backward-looking. They said little about their own time other than that it was a time of nostalgia. Regrettably, the firm which was founded to bring fine design within the reach of all ended up by supplying finely made obsolete furniture to the very rich. Only William Morris's own designs for wallpapers and fabrics reached a wider public and then only a public already interested in the arts.

Two developments in the period 1830–70 were especially important in the history of western furniture; one concerns production and marketing methods, the other the number of jobs a piece of furniture could be expected to perform. From the 1850s Michael Thonet's factory in Vienna was producing elegant and very cheap bentwood furniture. Chairs by him or by his imitators formed the basic furnishing of many European cafés until after World War II. Thonet's marketing originality, (successfully copied on a large scale in the 1950s), was to produce all the components for a piece of furniture and send them to be assembled in the country for which they were destined.

Dual use furniture had existed since Medieval times, the 16th-century chair-table in England and North America being one example. The 19th-century love of gadgetry and experiment resulted in a steady stream of patent furniture which sometimes served a useful purpose, sometimes not. It is, for example, difficult to understand the functional reasoning behind the American piano which turned into a bed. In patent seat furniture functional thinking is usually clear. As early as the Regency period in England armchairs had been made with a back that could be made to recline into two or three positions and a foot that could rise to provide a base for a semi-reclining posture. In the mid-century large numbers of variations on this, including

An example of bentwood furniture, the upright chair known as Thonet no. 14. First produced in 1859, it has been manufactured ever since, and millions of examples have been made.

A chair designed by Belter, made and carved in solid rosewood, which he often used. It is a florid Neo-Rococo in style, with curly acanthus, C-shaped scrolls and other motifs. The shape is exaggerated.

chairs working on a ratchet, were patented, as were swing chairs and swivel chairs. Although this outburst of inventiveness may have been due to the growing speed of life and business much patent furniture was probably purely the result of a fascination with mechanical contrivances.

1870–1918 Eclecticism continued to be the keynote of commercial production in the 1870s and 1880s. In France during the Second Empire (1852–70) reproduction First Empire furniture was fashionable as was the reproduction of Louis XIV and XV styles. When the Second Empire ended reminders of the Napoleonic dynasty fell from favor for 20 years; but over-stuffed

chairs and sofas with a haphazard mixture of motifs borrowed from the reigns of the last three pre-Revolutionary Louis continued to be popular. Cane furniture also continued to be made and porcelain, gilt bronze, brass and rosewoods were combined in a way which suggested that amongst the wealthy aesthetic tastes were omnivorous.

Eastlake's *Hints on Household Taste* which first appeared in 1868 and was frequently reprinted during the following decade, points to a similarly confused situation in England. The United States responded to the work with approval, and a confusion of Gothic and Romanesque ornament was accepted there too.

Outside the main stream of commercial developments completely different thoughts about furniture were being expressed. William Morris's firm had created an interest in old handicrafts. Before his death in

An ebonized sideboard designed by E. W. Godwin c1867. The thin supporting members were to be taken up and trivialized in the Japanese revival furniture of Western Europe in the later 19th century. Here, however, they express a genuine aesthetic.

1896 his firm had made quantities of relatively cheap wooden rush-bottom chairs and bedroom furniture. The Arts and Crafts Movement, inspired by Morris, was formed by a later generation of designers and craftsmen. In 1888 the Arts and Crafts Exhibition Society held its first exhibition. The most important members of the Society included Voysey, Ashbee and Mackmurdo. Ashbee's work reflects the rural element in the Arts and Crafts Movement. Mackmurdo's domestic oak furniture of the 1880s exemplifies Morris's notion of the dignity of labor together with the beauty and social value of handmade work. Mackmurdo also produced other kinds of work. For some large-scale pieces he favored early Italian Renaissance shapes. At the end of the 19th century he designed a writing desk on which are painted Art Nouveau tulips. Voysey had a predilection for using long thin columns as supports for his cabinet furniture. In this he was probably influenced by the furniture of E. W. Godwin, who, in the 1860s and 1870s had independently created furniture based on Japanese styles in which fine wooden poles support cupboards and drawers.

Charles Rennie Mackintosh, a Scottish designer, also used long thin members for furniture. But whereas both Godwin and Voysey had considered function of primary importance, Mackintosh thought first of appearance. Function came a long way behind. His chairs, with their low wide seats and enormously high, thin backs resemble prie-dieux for giants. Between 1890 and 1910 he produced a range of seat, table and storage furniture of which much is of poor quality craftsmanship but which was found visually exciting at the time. Exhibited at the Vienna Sezession Mackintosh's work was a powerful stimulus to the Art Nouveau movement.

A chair designed by Charles Rennie Mackintosh in 1901–2 which shows his preference for elongated forms. The seat is too low for comfort but enhances the height of the back. The thin side pieces recall Godwin's Japanese-influenced sideboard. The painted decoration is pure Art Nouveau.

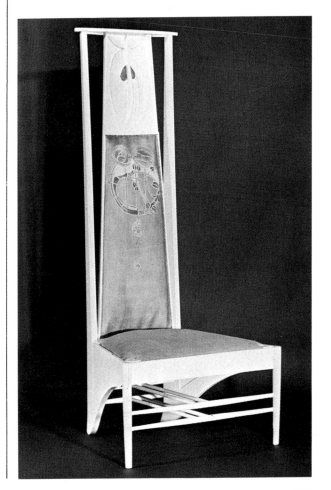

Left: A table designed by Stephen Webb, c1900, probably one of the most underrated of English cabinet-designers. The quality of the decoration with its delicate engraved ivory inlay is high. In shape the piece derives from the Rococo period. The designs of Jean Bérain, from an earlier period, may have influenced the inlay.

Right: A reconstruction of the *Pavillion des Arts Décoratifs*, one of the stands in the 1900 Universal Exhibition which was held in Paris. The furniture is by Louis Majorelle. The plant forms of the table in the foreground, and the elastic-looking sweep of the piano supports, and of the side of the chair on the left, are two of the hallmarks of French Art Nouveau.

It was not only in Britain that eclecticism brought a reaction. In Poland in the 1880s and 1890s the Cracow workshops, a group similar to the Arts and Crafts Movement, advocated a remodeled folk style, called the "Zakopane style". In France the *Union Centrale des Beaux-Arts appliqués à l'Industrie* of 1865 (later called the *Union Centrale des Arts décoratifs*) had social and aesthetic purposes close to those of Morris's followers.

From Mackmurdo, Voysey and Mackintosh in Britain, from Van de Velde in Belgium and the paintings of Gustav Klimt in Vienna; above all from the decadent movement of the 1890s in English and French literature and interior decoration, emerged the furniture of Art Nouveau. As in painting and literature it was a European dead end.

Art Nouveau has sometimes been regarded as the precursor of the Modern Movement. It is more nearly the last fling of Rococo. The tight, light curves of

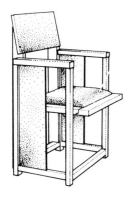

Above: A chair designed by Frank Lloyd Wright, in 1904.

Above right: An oak armchair by Ernest Gimson, c1905. The design draws on English country traditions, but there is nothing rustic about the delicate graduation of the size of the back slats or the modulation of the arm thickness.

Left: An extravagant piece of Art Nouveau furniture, this display cabinet was made by Gaudi c1900. It is of partly gilt walnut with a glass door divided by carved walnut curtains. The carving is mainly of sinuous vegetable shapes. Peacocks are engraved on the doors, a favorite Art Nouveau motif.

Rococo become flaccid in it. Vivacity is replaced by a languid elegance. Wood is used as though it were a substance capable of being melted and poured, as can be seen in the work of Emile Gallé, the glass and furniture designer, and of his acquaintance, Majorelle. In Belgium the architect Victor Horta and the designer Henri Van de Velde planned the furniture for complete rooms as composite works of art. In Horta's work the sinuous line of Art Nouveau was as tendril-like as in Gallé but Van de Velde gave greater tautness to his line by planning the overall design of each piece and subordinating decorative detail to the plan. In Spain the architect Antonio Gaudi designed a few pieces of furniture as outré as his architecture. In Munich August Endell designed serviceable furniture with a topping of Art Nouveau decoration.

Three escapes were attempted from the cul-de-sac of Art Nouveau. In England the spiritual descendants of the Arts and Crafts movement put their faith in maintaining the ancient crafts and in a rather naïve respect for materials, as the best craftsmen of the village tradition had done. Excellent work was carried out, particularly by Ernest Gimson and the Barnsleys. English oak and

219

walnut were the preferred woods. The movement still finds adherents and well-made handicrafts are produced but the maintenance of a peasant craftsman idiom in an industrial urban society seems both artificial and irrelevant. A similar experiment in Scandinavia in the 20th century has been successful because it harnessed a living tradition. In England the social message of Morris and the Arts and Crafts Movement was taken up by Roger Fry when he began the Omega workshop in 1913. Unfortunately, Fry's insistence that all Omega work should be anonymous alienated the artists who had joined him. His lack of business skills made the undertaking financially unsound and his designers, who included Vanessa Bell, Duncan Grant and Henri Gaudier-Brzeska, were painters and sculptors, not craftsmen. Consequently Omega furniture was attractively decorated but usually badly made.

The second escape was also tried in England and throughout the Western world. It accounts for the greater part of the well-made furniture produced before World War II, and still thrives. The style combined a conventional use of fine woods with outlines based on aristocratic or middle-class shapes and motifs of earlier periods, particularly those of 18th-century England. Ernest Gimson produced work of this kind, as did the firm of Gillow. Ambrose Heal designed pieces for his company which combine a traditional approach to shape and materials with a well thought out functionalism. The firm of Libertys, on the other hand, chose to copy a much earlier period; for a while in the 1880s a fashion arose for pseudo-Egyptian furniture. Other firms favored "free Renaissance" designs. This avenue of escape was clearly another fall into eclecticism.

The third attempt to evolve a new style began in the United States and Scandinavia. Frank Lloyd Wright looked at the functions required of a chair or a table as part of an architectural whole. The result was aesthetically pleasing but the function of individual pieces of furniture was sometimes sacrificed to the overall appearance of a room. In Denmark Kaare Klint adopted a similar approach but regarded furniture as purely functional leaving larger aesthetic considerations to the architect with whom he was working. His solutions to the problems of furniture design can more properly be considered as part of 20th-century history. They are the source from which much 20th-century thinking in the applied arts springs.

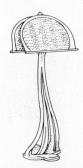

Music stand resembles an exotic plant with a great pod-shaped head.

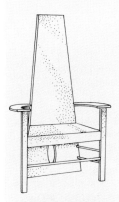

Height and thinness were exaggerated for elegant effect.

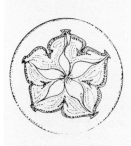

Flower designs, if not elongated, still distorted.

Plant forms were an obsession of Art Noveau, sweeping lines too.

Thin lines, wavey decoration and attenuated elegance mark Art Nouveau furniture. There were no significant advances in techniques or in the basic structure and function of furniture, though woodwork became sinuous. Functional thinking sometimes disappeared altogether. Abstract designs based on interweaving lines were popular and the influence of Anglo-Saxon and Celtic work is clear. Painted decorations on furniture were often of human figures, usually nude or dressed in floating draperies and dancing.

Exoticism: Far Eastern elements in the screen, Chinese influence on the sideboard.

Parts of furniture were non-functional such as the leaf like top.

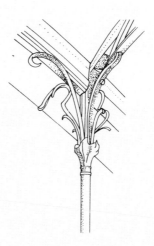

Pillars become tendrils, gas brackets hang down like predatory insects.

MODERN FURNITURE

By the early 1900s furniture designers were working to evolve new styles that would suit the conditions of contemporary living. The exotic element of Art Nouveau made it foreign to this idea. Rustic furniture had reached its limits.

In the 20th century furniture designs have changed more rapidly than ever before. The technology which has made such rapid changes possible has also provoked radical thought about the function and nature of furniture itself. Parallel with the development of new forms, though, runs a contrary movement. The late 19th-century revolt against industrialization emerged in the Arts and Crafts movement fostered by William Morris in England and the Zakopane movement in Poland. New technology and old style craftsmanship have sometimes worked together in harmony, and sometimes opposed one another.

1918–1945 Much machine-made furniture is of poor quality, because it is intended to be cheap, or of poor design because it follows, at however great a distance, a form designed for production by hand. The cream-painted, white-wood bedroom suite with gilt plastic, pseudo Rococo handles to the drawers, and the bare

A chaise-longue designed by Le Corbusier in 1927. Though spare in design, it is also an extremely comfortable piece of furniture.

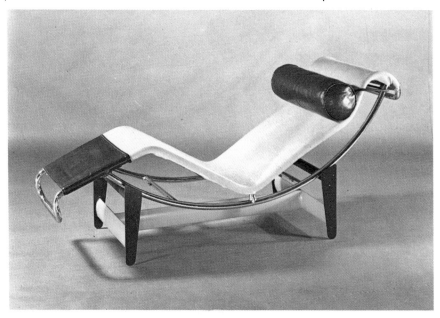

The "Barcelona chair", designed by Mies van der Rohe, so-called because it was designed for the German pavilion at the 1929 World Exhibition in Barcelona. It consists of intersecting steel bars, with leather cushions supported on leather straps.

pine chest of drawers copied from a provincial pattern which has been dead for 60 or 70 years are examples of styles which continue to be seen all too often. Walter Gropius, Director of the Bauhaus until 1930, summed up the essential weakness of such design for industrial production when he said that the "illogical machine imitation of hand-made goods infallibly bears the stamp of a make-shift substitute." The standardization of furniture types, usually considered essential for factory production, may have been in the mind of Le Corbusier, the architect and designer, when he declared that all furniture can be reduced to cases, seats and tables. Besides breaking down the range of furniture to basic types, he also reduced traditional forms to their essentials, stripping away all applied decoration in accordance with his concept of the house as a "machine for living in." However, his chaise-longue of 1927 acts as a corrective to the ascetic vision raised by this term, and indicates why his furniture is so much more satisfactory than that produced by many of his imitators. The "machine for living in" must encourage people to live in it. The furniture needs to be comfortable.

The Bauhaus has gained the reputation of being the most influential center of design in the 20th century. The truth of this should not blind us to a weakness in its aim. Our society needs to mass-produce finely designed objects, whereas the founding thesis of the Bauhaus was as much a return to handicrafts as was William Morris's movement, despite the difference in the materials used. The most interesting furniture to emerge from the Bauhaus was the work of Marcel Breuer and Mies van der Rohe, following Mart Stamm's invention of the steel cantilever chair in 1924. Breuer and van der Rohe each produced a chair formed from a single loop of tubing. Tubular steel was a remarkable innovation, since it was extremely strong and pliant. The most successful variant on this theme was Breuer's version which first appeared in 1928 and went into production at the Thonet factory in 1934. Mies van der Rohe's most prestigious piece of furniture was his steel and leather chair for the German pavilion at the 1929 World Exhibition in Barcelona. The extreme simplicity of the form is deceptive. This piece looks as though it is purely machine made, and must lend itself to mass production. However, its elegance is at least partly due to skilled finishing and it is assuredly a luxury product. This is an example of the paradox of fine 20th-century design; the methods of industrial production have been used, not to mass-produce furniture, but to exploit the aesthetic advantages of perfectly cut ma-

A chair by Marcel Breuer, revealing the contemporary concern for stripping furniture to its essentials, using the simplest undecorated forms to meet a functional need. The piece is constructed from just four pieces of plywood.

A collection of furniture by Rietveld. Each chair and table is seen as an abstractly related series of angles and planes, not as a solution to a functional problem. In the table in the foreground the dominance of the sculptural idea over the functional is apparent.

terials. Mies van der Rohe was interested in solutions to individual problems in architecture and furniture rather than in solving the problems of mass-production.

A completely different objective was held by the members of the de Stijl movement in Holland, which set out to produce abstract work. Its members were opposed, they declared, to "Modern Baroque." Their weapons were to be "the logical principle of a maturing style based on purer relationships with the spirit of our times and our means of expression." Forms were to be non-functional. Oddly enough their non-functionality as furniture ánd their validity as sculpture make the works of Rietveld (the only furniture designer of the movement) the spiritual descendants of Brustolon's High Baroque extravaganzas for Pietro Venier.

In the 18th and 19th centuries fine furniture design and construction in the Scandinavian countries was deeply indebted to France and England. In the 20th century it became the turn of Scandinavia to influence

MODERN

good design in Western Europe and throughout the Western World. The central concern of English 18th-century craftsmanship is still apparent: the concentration on finely related proportions. It is combined with a native tradition of using local woods, particularly birch, in a simple way.

Kaare Klint, in Denmark, pioneered this style. He was no revolutionary. It was part of his creed always to examine the work of the past to see what answers had previously been found to individual problems. The craftsmanship he employed was traditional, but his conception of furniture was new. He studied it completely rationally, seeing it as the attempt to provide solutions to a series of problems raised by specific everyday requirements. For example, before designing a sideboard he researched into the quantities of cutlery, table-linen, glass and crockery stored by the average Danish middle-class family, and considered the different dimensions of plates, glasses, knives and other items of tableware. From these figures he established the necessary sizes of compartments. The sideboard which finally emerged is elegant and spare in line. Its apparent lack of cubic capacity is belied by the amount its rationally organized interior spaces hold.

Klint worked as the furniture designer associate of the architect Carl Petersen until becoming first Professor of Furniture Design in the Copenhagen Academy of Fine Arts in 1924. This position gave him the chance to preach his gospel of rationalizing furniture design and of making furniture which fulfilled a function as precisely as possible. One of his great innovations was to standardize chair and table heights and drawer sizes.

Other Scandinavian designers used traditional materials but applied new and revolutionary techniques to them. Wood was the predominant material. Alvar Aalto in Finland had a particular liking for Finnish birch. His laminated armchairs are extremely stylish, the cantilevered laminated frame being well related to the curved plywood seat back to please the eye as well as the body. In the 1930s he produced simple tables and stacking stools in which the top is supported by legs whose bases are solid birch but whose upper sections are inwardly curving laminations. The Swede Karl Bruno Mathsson also used curved laminations as table supports and was one of the first people to make furniture to which other pieces could be added to

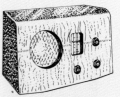

In response to new technology a new piece of furniture appeared, the radio cabinet. Characteristic geometric design.

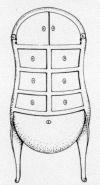

Colored and embossed leather were popular as decoration on fine furniture.

Massive and monumental shapes resemble architecture but are not functional. Round ends a common feature.

ART DECO

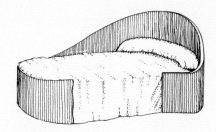

Fashionable beds were often circular or kidney-shaped and sometimes had upholstered headboards.

Art Deco reintroduced old techniques of furniture decoration such as lacquer, stamped and colored leather and fine veneerings, and produced at least two new ones, in the use of shagreen and mirror glass to cover wooden surfaces. Forms were stylized, often geometrical, and, as the style developed, became monumental. Three new types of furniture evolved, the cocktail cabinet, the radio cabinet and the radio gramophone. Off-white was an especially fashionable color for interior decoration and furniture.

Many pieces were simplified versions of French Rococo, unfrivolous, severely balanced.

Some furniture was made completely of glass.

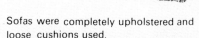

Sofas were completely upholstered and loose cushions used.

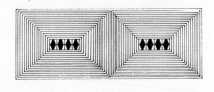

Common motifs: Stylized flowers and leaves; interwoven figures forming a geometric pattern; patterns distantly resembling rows of flowers; purely geometric abstract designs.

transform a simple piece of furniture into a more luxurious one as the buyer became more affluent.

A few Scandinavian and German ideas found their way into other parts of Europe between the wars. This occurred in several ways: through the agency of exhibitions such as the Swedish Exhibition held in London in 1930; through the influence of small magazines and a few fervent admirers; through refugees like Marcel Breuer who, in the mid-1930s, designed furniture in England for Isokon and Heals; and through firms like Isokon and, for metal furniture, PEL (Practical Equipment Limited). There is however a difference between the original ideas of the Bauhaus, which were for mass-produced cheap furniture (even though some of the best work of Bauhaus designers was expensive) and the concept of well-designed metal furniture in England, which was always intended to be highly modish and costly. One of Sir Herbert Read's criticisms of a steel chair by Sir Ambrose Heal, exhibited in 1935, was that whereas he considered that a steel chair by Breuer produced commercially would retail at two guineas, the Heal chair was priced at ten. He had, in a sense, missed the point. The Heal chair, which is distantly based on a Roman curule chair, is quite clearly meant to be an "objet de luxe". It is also a fine example of the style now labeled "Art Deco".

Furniture by Aalto. The armchair on the right is of bent plywood slung between supports of laminated birch. The other chairs are designed on a similar principle but are upholstered. The small table in the foreground shows the care with which Aalto integrated solid and laminated wood in order to achieve a satisfying line between table leg and table top.

This macassar ebony table, designed by Ruhlmann between 1930 and 1932 displays the elegance of his best work. Despite its late date it has none of the monumentality which marked much of Ruhlmann's furniture in this period. The sweep of the supports, the simple brass binding to the feet and the perfect workmanship and proportions combine to produce a sense of lightness and stylishness.

Art Deco which can be dated from c1920 to the mid 1930s has recently become fashionable again. Unfortunately it is its mass- or factory-produced articles that are best known because they are more plentiful than "one-off" pieces. The real craftsmanship of the best Art Deco furniture is still known in the main only to those fortunate enough to own original work by the great craftsmen of the 1920s and 1930s. Of all Art Deco designers probably the best was Emile-Jacques Ruhlmann, and Paris, where he worked, was the center of the fine furniture-making trade of the Art Deco period. Ruhlmann, like many of the major designers of his time, was an interior decorator. He planned rooms in which he included his own furniture together with works by other people from different branches of the fine and applied arts. His work was very expensive indeed. He used only the best materials and demanded the highest standard of craftsmanship from the men who worked for him. During the early 1920s his furniture was usually delicate in design but for the last five or six years of his life (he died in 1933) it became more monumental in scale. For beds he favored variations on the box or boat-shaped Empire bed, but without the canopy. His dressing tables and ladies' desks are either very simple with straight legs and an oval mirror or, as a gentle variation, they have a very slightly curved edge, often picked out with a strip of ivory. Ivory tips to the legs act as feet. Ruhlmann's chairs owe much to 18th- and

MODERN

A 1930s English suburban lounge, which displays a fondness for dully patterned objects (the armchairs) against a neutral ground (the plain walls). The furniture is of a pale wood, which was popular. The mirror over the fireplace, the wall-lights, cigarette stand, standard lamp, china cabinet and large television set with the small screen are all now popularly associated with 1930s English furniture.

MODERN

early 19th-century models. Much simplified variations of the *bergère* or of Empire *fauteuils* appear in his work. His favorite woods were macassar ebony and Caucasian burr walnut. For decorative details ivory, silver, silvered bronze and shagreen were preferred. Upholstery was usually either velvet or brocade. It was often specially designed and made for an individual piece or pieces of furniture and for the room of which they were to form a part.

Lacquer came back into fashion but usually with non-oriental-inspired motifs. The Japanese artist Sugawara taught true oriental lacquer techniques to, amongst others, Jean Dunand and Eileen Grey. Their work is perhaps the finest European lacquer ever produced. Dunand, a French designer, was primarily a metalworker, and his early works in lacquer were for small boxes and umbrella handles. He later produced magnificent lacquer screens, panels to be incorporated in furniture designed by others, including Ruhlmann, and indeed panels to cover whole walls and doors in the French liner "Normandie" in 1935.

Eileen Grey was an English architect, interior decorator and furniture designer who worked in Paris. Whereas Dunand was at times inspired by the oriental derivation of lacquer, Eileen Grey used it as a new material, and her motifs, certainly not Eastern in origin, cannot accurately be described as "Art Deco" or "Modernist". The third major lacquerer of the period in Paris was Japanese, Katsu Hamanaka and, as might be expected, his screens show their oriental origin in the motifs employed and more importantly in the disposition of images in space. The relationship between the image and its surroundings recalls the great screens of the Japanese 18th century. He also made lacquer furniture which, in shape, is purely European.

A relatively simple division can be made in France between Modernist (followers of the Bauhaus, Mies van der Rohe, Marcel Breuer and others) and Art Deco furniture designers as defined at their extremes by Le Corbusier and Ruhlmann. No such distinction can be made in England. Perhaps the English furniture designer who most resembles Ruhlmann (at least in the wealth of his clients, and so in his freedom to use expensive materials) was Alistair Maynard. Since, however, even the "best" furniture in England remained closer in quality and price to that bought by the ordinarily well-off, his furniture was far less opulent

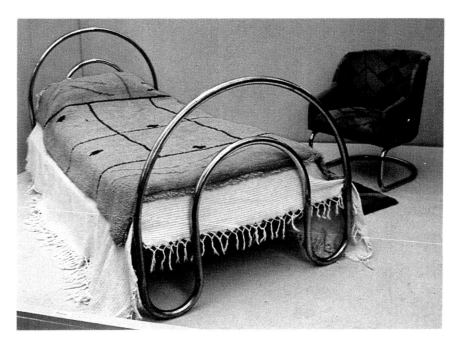

Practical Equipment Limited (PEL) pioneered the production of tubular steel furniture in England. The semicircular motif of the bed, made sometime between 1932 and 1936, is derived from Art Deco but the style has become functional and spare. Both bed and chair, however, show an attention to attractiveness and comfort sometimes lacking in "functional" furniture.

than that of Ruhlmann. In France there was a far greater distinction between the rich and the rest. The designs of Serge Chermayeff, R. W. Symonds and Robert Lutyens in 1930s England are for solid bourgeois furniture. They share the Art Deco interest in geometric shapes, particularly the semi-circle and the quadrant, but for them it was simply an interest not an obsession.

One of the striking features of 1930s furniture in Europe is that there are few right angle edges. A sideboard, a table, a bed or a dressing table may be rectangular but its edges or ends are usually rounded. Another characteristic feature was of decoration. This was either of purely geometrical patterning and almost always asymmetrical if complex, or it employed shells, flowers or oddly archaic looking human figures.

Wood or metal remained the customary materials for furniture but glass became very popular in the 1930s. All-glass furniture was very rare, also no doubt very uncomfortable and very expensive. The French designer René Lalique made a few all-glass dining tables c1930. Pilkington Brothers exhibited a glass bedroom in 1933 but it was solely for advertisement. The Frenchman Pierre Legrain made a glass and stainless steel piano. More often glass was used in a conven-

MODERN

Some examples of the British Utility range of furniture, 1946. The dressing table and stool are severely functional, designed to use the minimum of timber. Their design is also as simple as possible to save valuable craftsmen's time in assembling the pieces. Nevertheless, they achieve a kind of elegant solidity.

tional way, combined with other materials. It became especially popular in the form of mirror glass and everything, from bedside tables to writing desks, dining tables, chests of drawers and the newly created cocktail cabinet were covered in it. The glare in a well-lit fashionable room with many such pieces must have been disturbing. So too must the surrealist sense of glimpsing odd bits of your body as you moved around the room.

The vast majority of furniture produced between the wars, however, was neither Modernist nor Art Deco. The growth of American affluence and the social revolution that took place in Europe during World War I led to an enormous expansion of a working- and lower-middle-class clientele for larger quantities of factory-made furniture. The ability of the affluent middle class to maintain large houses, particularly in cities, declined, as women who before the war would have worked as servants took up factory employment. The market for good-quality expensive ready-made furniture which was yet outside the luxury class correspondingly fell. In particular there was no longer any market at all for furniture which was not relatively easy to keep clean and tidy. This was not true of furniture at the cheap end of the market. Women who before the war would have "gone into service" were used to hard work and now wanted furniture which as nearly as possible resembled the furniture of the grand. In England a Neo-Jacobean and Neo-Elizabethan boom set in; only slightly less popular was reproduction Queen Anne. France adopted Neo-Rococo. The USA found all four attractive. Some more adventurous spirits in the 1930s wanted to emulate the "modern" life-style of the bright young things of the 1920s. For them a cheapened "Modernism" appeared. This usually meant that extraneous chrome fittings were added to otherwise ordinary pieces of furniture, or, in the case of chests-of-drawers, a few of the drawers were put on stilts to give the piece a lop-sided look.

The most important pre-war developments to affect furniture production after World War II were in materials not styles. Plastic had been invented by an Englishman in 1855. The first completely synthetic plastic suitable for commercial production was patented by a Belgian in 1909 and called "Bakelite". It was strong enough for small items like desk- and table-ware but brittle. In the 1920s production of plastics grew enormously. However it was research directed at war production and the attempts to find synthetic, light materials strong enough to support weight, and capable of being easily and rapidly molded that led to the invention of plastics suitable for furniture. Before the war the most commonly employed plastic was a rigid laminate: Formica. Invented in the United States in 1913, Formica is made of two resins bonded together and is usually backed by plywood. It was revolutionary. The surface is waterproof, heat-resistant and almost proof against scratching. It was used for table tops and remains a major boon to café proprietors and those doing housework.

Great Britain's one real contribution to furniture design in the mid-20th century was forced upon her. With the outbreak of war in 1939 most furniture factories were closed. The craftsmen were required for munitions work or for service in the armed forces. Timber, of which England produced very little, was in short supply and those factories which remained open for furniture production lacked raw materials. In 1942 the Utility

MODERN

Furniture Scheme was introduced. Specified factories were to make furniture and, in order to control the use of scarce craftsmanship and raw materials and in order to regulate prices, strict restraints were introduced. All designs were standardized. The tradition of deceptive simplicity exemplified by Ernest Gimson at the beginning of the century and continued in the 1920s and 1930s by some of the designs of Gordon and W. H. Russell was exchanged for a true simplicity. Design was of a high caliber, particularly for bedroom furniture, and the standard of construction was high. Upholstered furniture, although well-designed, was less successful because of the discrepancy between poor quality cloth and meager appearance with the purpose of upholstery: to add luxury and comfort to an object. The contribution of Utility furniture was that it introduced, albeit by duress, good simple design into the houses of many people in the United Kingdom who otherwise would never have considered it, and it may, thereby, have done a useful job of visual education.

Jacobsen's swan chair, first made in 1958. This light, bird-like form is an example of the developing romanticism of furniture in the 1950s and 1960s. It was made originally for a hotel in Copenhagen and is one example of the collaboration between Jacobsen the designer and Fritz Hansen's firm of furniture makers.

An ottoman and armchair by Charles Eames. Both pieces are in rosewood veneer over molded plywood upholstered in latex foam and (usually artificial) leather. They reproduce in 1956 terms the masculine comfort of the English club armchair. The swivel chair, however, gives greater mobility and the whole form is lighter.

1948–1978   In the post-war world three countries, or groups of countries, have dominated furniture design: Scandinavia, Italy and the United States. Although Scandinavian design affected almost all the best factory-made furniture of the 1950s in the United States and Western Europe, the pieces of Scandinavian furniture most admired are often the product not of the factory system but of the small workshop. They are pieces which are hand-made and individually designed. The Scandinavian renaissance in furniture design began with Kaare Klint. During World War II his ideas were adopted by Børge Morgensen in Denmark. Morgensen was head of furniture design for the Danish Cooperative Society which in 1944 opened its first furniture shop in Copenhagen. Much of the best post-war Scandinavian furniture, however, has not been as rational as its parentage might presuppose. Hans Wegner, Finn Juhl and Arne Jacobsen have introduced sculptural, romantic, elements into it. Jacobsen's "Egg" chair is as much a sculpture as a piece of furniture and his "Swan" chair gives the impression of hovering gently above the ground.

The quality of design and craftsmanship in Scandi-

MODERN

navian furniture is the result of a close relationship between designer and maker. Each major designer works in association with a particular mastercraftsman and his workshop. Hans Wegner is usually associated with the mastercraftsman Johannes Hansen; Arne Jacobsen's works are carried out by the firm of Fritz Hansens.

Apart from the pioneering work of Frank Lloyd Wright the American commitment to modern design can be dated from 1940 when Charles Eames and Eero Saarinen won prizes in the competition for domestic design organized by the New York Museum of Modern Art. The chair with which Eames won was never produced commercially. By the time there was any possibility of manufacturing it America was at war and the welding process required to affix the aluminum legs was reserved for military projects. Eames was luckier in 1946 with his LCM chair. (The initials are simply a method of registration and have no meaning.) This chair for the first time used molded plywood for the back and seat to fit the seated human figure In 1948 Eames scored again with his DAR chair, in which glass fiber was used commercially for the first time. The shell of the chair can be mounted on a variety of plinths. By 1956 there was a new luxury in Eames' style. In that year he produced his lounge-chair and ottoman, which are clearly within the English tradition of deeply buttoned leather furniture of a very masculine elegance. The Eames chair strides out of its tradition because of its seeming lightness. The quality found in Jacobsen's work is once again apparent.

Another 1950s designer who showed the same desire to produce seemingly weightless work was Harry Bertoia. His wire mesh chairs mounted on a chromium-plated steel rod frame are delicately articulated pieces of sculpture. Their legs are so thin that the chair again seems to float. Unfortunately the wire motif was seized on by designers who did not understand the aesthetic underlying its use.

Consequently the 1950s saw the production of a mass of spindly metal furniture, usually with a colored knob on the end of each metal rod. Much of it was so shoddily constructed that it soon fell apart.

Bertoia was one of a number of fine designers for one of the two outstanding American furniture-making companies: Knoll Associates of New York. The other was Herman Miller Furniture Company of Michigan.

Above: wire range by
Bertoia, c1950.
Below: seating system
by Colombo, 1968.

MODERN

Almost all the great American furniture designers in the 20th century have worked for one or other of them. The list includes Mies van der Rohe, Charles Eames and Eero Saarinen.

Italy's influence on furniture-making was mainly a phenomenon of the 1960s and was apparent in two distinct fields. On the one hand a new urbanity, a "chic" element was introduced, which had not existed since the 1930s; on the other, at the lower end of the market Italian designers pioneered "fun furniture", like the "Sacco" chair by Piero Gatti, Cesare Paolini and Franco Teodoro. This was a synthetic leather bag part filled with granules of expanded polystyrene. For elegant furniture Gian Carlo Piretti, in 1969, designed "Plica", a folding chair of chrome-plated steel tubing with a back and seat of colored transparent plastic.

The great technical discovery of the 1960s with important consequences for design was represented in 1960 by Verner Panton's molded glass-fiber and polyester stacking chair (though it was not actually manufactured until 1967). For the first time the whole body of a chair could be produced by a single industrial process, eliminating the need for assembly. In the early 1970s the British invention of a method of making furniture whereby a core of rigid plastic and a covering

A collection of the furniture of Saarinen. The dining chair is an extremely elegant example of post-war design. The cast aluminum base supports on the thinnest of pedestals, like that of a wineglass, a molded plastic and fiberglass shell. The table base is of cast aluminum and the top is usually a plastic laminate.

A flat for a young couple, from the Formica firm. The chairs are extremely simple but built for comfort. The interior is designed as a single living unit, the storage furniture, tables and chairs being seen as forming a room together. The clean lines and simple, good proportions show the influence of Scandinavian hand-made furniture from early in the century.

of an upholstery plastic are produced together has taken "instant furniture" one stage further.

The problem of storage has been tackled in a new way since the war. Fixed cupboards, except where built-in, have become less popular. In their place designers have been creating units which can be set up, taken down and rearranged in a variety of ways. In 1948 the English designers Robin Day and Clive Latimer received awards for a plywood storage system slung on tubular metal supports. By 1968 Joe Colombo was able to produce his "Square Plastic System" in which the sections can be stacked, hung on a wall, be linked or placed back to back. Combinations of seat, storage and table units are now commonplace.

Flexibility is one of the key-notes of the design of the late 1960s and 1970s. Furniture which can be added to or taken apart and reassembled in another form dominates contemporary design. Change and rearrangement are seen as central to a contemporary way of life. Postures reflect this, and "soft" furniture, chairs which are little more than squidgy balloons which respond to every movement of the body and rearrange themselves in accordance with it, carry the reflection into furniture-making itself.

Next to flexibility there is a strong vein of romanticism in the furniture of the late 1960s and 1970s. The reversion in America and Britain to a rustic style in the 1960s is part of this, and is a movement which ex-

Chair designed by Ronald Koob, 1973. In the 1970s there has been a growing popularity for furniture which is both sculptural and flexible in the uses to which it can be put. This piece allows for assembly in a number of ways.

presses nostalgia. Another strand of romanticism is represented by the continuing use of bird forms in Arne Jacobsen's plastic swivel office armchair of 1968 and by the new literalism with which the human figure is treated in the creation of, at times, surreal seat furniture. Luigi Colani, Aage Egeriis and Angelo Mangianotti have all designed chairs which resemble the outline of a seated human being.

Further romantic overtones are present in the sense of movement and in the use of transparent materials in some modern furnishings. Plastics make possible the production of large objects, easily movable and almost unbreakable, in a material permeable by light. The aesthetic possibilities are enormous. In the US, John Mascheroni and in Great Britain Peter Hoyte, amongst many, have designed fine seat furniture using transparent acrylic plastics.

The impression of movement, caught at a moment in time, which appears in Jacobsen's work and in the stacking tables "Rotondo" of Cesare Leonardi and Franca Stagi is a sculptural quality shared by only a few pieces of furniture from the past. It is apparent in some Art Nouveau works, such as the plant forms used by Majorelle, but in those the movement was of slow organic growth. Nowaday, most of our furnishings are required to be capable of providing many shapes. However, as a point of stasis in the flux, some pieces are still needed to declare that from the flux a moment can be permanently retained.

Aalto, Hugo Alvar Henrik
b1899 Finnish architect and designer. Influenced by Mart Stamm's invention (1924) of cantilever tubular steel chair. Founded Artek firm in Helsinki (1933) to manufacture furnishings from own designs. Worked mainly in laminated birch plywood from 1930s. Success of designs rests in fine proportions and apparent simplicity, which lends them to factory reproduction.

Adam, Robert
1728–92 British architect and designer. Most influential Neoclassicist of 18th-century Britain. Designs show understanding of Roman ornament. He influenced later designs of Thomas Chippendale the Elder, particularly for Nostell Priory, Harewood House (Yorks); Kenwood House, London.

Belter, John Henry
1804–63 American. b Germany; settled New York, 1844. Designed and produced in own factory opulent and over-decorated neo-Rococo furniture mainly in black walnut or rosewood, for which he invented a form of lamination enabling the wood to be shaped and carved.

Bérain, Jean
1640–1711. French decorator, stage and furniture designer. Designs (of elaborate, organized series of curling tendrils and leaves enclosing tiny scenes of apes, monkeys and grotesques) adopted by Boulle and through him became the standard form of surface decoration for furniture throughout Europe. Later in the 18th century these formed the major influence on the development of Rococo.

Bonzanigo, Giuseppe Maria
1745–1820 Italian designer and craftsman. Worked in Turin after 1773 making furniture, much for the Piedmontese Royal Palace. Official Woodcarver to the Crown 1787. Furniture remarkable for virtuoso carving; style spirited Rococo, or modified Neoclassical.

Boulle, André-Charles
1642–1732 French. First great French *ébéniste*. Best known for inlaid work in ebony, tortoiseshell, brass and pewter, with fine gilt-bronze mounts, *Ébeniste du roi* 1672 on. Much of his output commissioned for Louis XIV. Furniture made in the "Boulle style" until end 19th century.

Breuer, Marcel Lajos
b1902 Hungarian. Studied and taught at the Bauhaus under Gropius. From the 1930s in Berlin, England, and since 1937 in the US has worked mainly in tubular steel. Responsible for some of the best design in industrially produced furniture.

Brustolon, Andrea
1662–1732 Italian sculptor and designer. Lived in Belluno, where he worked on ecclesiastical and lay commissions. Worked in Venice c1677–99. Responsible for design and execution of probably the most magnificent Baroque suite of furniture in the city for Pietro Venier. Lacquered and enameled furniture in boxwood really sculpture.

Carlin, Martin
d1785 French cabinet-maker. Worked mainly for Parisian *marchands-merciers*. Work a very feminine version of the Neoclassicism of the Louis XVI style; often includes decorative plaques of painted Sèvres porcelain. Gilt-bronze mounts shaped like swags of drapery a common feature.

Chippendale, Thomas the Elder
1718–79 Best known 18th-century British furniture designer, maker and supplier. Fame rests on *The Gentleman and Cabinet-Maker's Directory* (first ed. 1754, 2nd ed. 1755 and 3rd extended ed. published in parts 1759–62). A guide to furniture he supplied. Designs in the first edition in prevailing Rococo taste (including Chinese and Gothic) unoriginal. The third edition added Neoclassical pieces; some of the finest

MAKERS AND DESIGNERS

pieces from the Chippendale workshop are in Neoclassical style. Besides elaborate and costly work his firm made large quantities of relatively cheap, simple furniture of very high quality. The firm was carried on after his death by his son, *Thomas Chippendale the Younger* c1749–1822, who possibly designed the Neoclassical work.

Colombo, Joe
1930–71. Italian architect and furniture designer. Major designs include a comprehensive system of living units, an extremely versatile series of demountable plastic storage units and the first plastic chair to be made in a single process by injection moulding.

Conran, Terence
b1931 British designer and manufacturer of a wide range of household goods, responsible for making available modern designs at low cost in Britain in the 1960s and 1970s through his marketing stores: *Habitat*.

Cressent, Charles
1685–1758 French sculptor and *ébéniste*. Greatest furniture designer and maker of the Regency. Until late 1740s work distinguished by superbly sculpted ormolu mounts over plain wood veneers. Later he abandoned elaborate mounts and turned to floral marquetry. *Ébéniste* to the Regent 1719 on.

Cucci, Domenico
1635–1704/5 Italian sculptor and furniture maker. Employed exclusively 1660–83 by Louis XIV. Made some of the most sumptuous palace furniture ever produced, using ebony, panels of *pietre dure*, gilding and ormolu. Possibly the most masterly Baroque furniture maker of 17th-century France.

Cuvilliés, François the Elder
1695–1768 Walloon-born architect and designer. Apart from 1720–24 when he studied architecture in Paris, from 1706 he lived at the Bavarian court in Munich. Responsible for the finest Bavarian Rococo palace interiors, including the Amalienburg and Munich Residenz.

Dagly, Gerhard
c1653–after 1714 Born Spa (now in Belgium). Finest of European 17th- and 18th-century lacquer makers. Worked for Friedrich Wilhelm of Brandenburg 1687–1713. He worked both in the conventional black, red and gold lacquers and in a white lacquer, superficially resembling porcelain.

Du Cerceau, Jacques Androuet
c1520–c1584 French designer and ornamentalist. The first to publish c1550 a series of designs for beds, cabinets and tables, overloaded with Renaissance ornament. No examples of most extreme designs exist; less elaborate pieces influenced by him survive.

Eames, Charles
1907–1978 American furniture designer. Responsible for some of the finest and most technically advanced 20th-century design. Produced: 1946 – the two-part plywood dining chair; 1957 – armchair and footstool of laminated rosewood and anodized aluminum; jointly with Saarinen in 1940 – the first standardized series of storage units based on readily available industrial products.

Eastlake, Charles Lock
1836–1906 English architect and writer on design. His *Hints on Household Taste in Furniture, Upholstery and other Details* (1868) was immensely influential on English and American taste. Book describes the general contemporary Gothic style.

Gaudreaux, Antoine Robert
c1680–1751 French Regency and Rococo cabinet-maker. Worked for Louis XV and Mme de Pompadour. Designed furniture, magnificent in both materials and craftsmanship. Caffieri, the greatest maker of Rococo ormolu, made some of his mounts.

Goddard, John
c1723–85 American. One of the most important members of the related Goddard and Townsend families, the great furniture-making dynasties of Newport, Rhode Island. Furniture elegant but solid and unpretentious. Mahogany work excellent.

Haupt, Georg
1741–84 Swedish cabinet-maker. Worked in Paris and London, then became cabinet-maker to the King of Sweden. Best-known 18th-century Swedish craftsman. Work is in the Louis XVI style.

Hepplewhite, George
d1786 English furniture designer. Served apprenticeship to Gillow of Lancaster. Set up as a furniture designer in London c1760. No furniture by him is known but *The Cabinet-Maker and Upholsterer's Guide* (1788, revised 1789 and 1794) assembled the fashionable elements of Adam's Neoclassicism and welded them into an elegant and unified whole. The book was intended for ordinary craftsmen, to aid production of Neoclassically inspired furniture elegantly and simply.

Hope, Thomas
1769–1831 English gentleman archeologist and furniture designer. *Household Furniture and Decoration*, designs in Grecian and Egyptian styles, published 1807, influenced English Regency furniture to greater archeological exactness than contemporary French Empire style.

Hoppenhaupt, Johann Michael
1709–1755 German furniture designer. His Rococo ornament fantastic and exotic. From 1740 worked for Frederick the Great in Berlin under Nahl. In 1746 became *Directeur des Ornements*. Designs published 1751–55. Adopted ideas from Cuvilliés but work more exaggerated. Motifs include swans, chinamen, dragons.

Jacob, Georges
1739–1814 French *menuisier*. Worked in Louis XV, Louis XVI, Directory and Empire styles. Virtually invented the form of the Louis XVI chair. Introduced plain mahogany for chairs to France. During French Revolution made furniture to the designs of Percier and Fontaine for the government. Retired 1796, when sons *Georges II* 1768–1803 and *François-Honoré Georges* 1770–1841 took over the business. Called themselves "Jacob Frères". In 1800 Georges returned to work. In 1803 he became his remaining son's partner; renamed "Jacob Desmalter et Cie". They produced the finest *menuiserie* and *ébénisterie* of the French Empire.

Jacobsen, Arne
1902–71 Danish architect and furniture designer. Most famous in particular for seat furniture designs of highly sculptural quality, in particular "Egg" and "Swan" chairs of the 1950s.

Johnson, Thomas
1714–78 English furniture designer and craftsman. Published designs for highly complicated Rococo decorative pieces (mirror frames, candlestands etc). No seat or case furniture.

Juhl, Finn
b1912 Danish architect and furniture designer. Designs are sculptural, yet give the impression of extreme simplicity. Detail is impeccable and demands a high standard of craftsmanship, met by Niels Vodder, the master-craftsman whose workshop carries out most of Juhl's work.

Juvarra, Filippo
1678–1736 Sicilian architect and furniture designer. Worked in the royal palaces of Piedmont and Spain. Furniture highly flamboyant, brilliantly colored and heavily patterned Rococo. Lacks the delicacy of French or German Rococo but has tremendous vitality.

MAKERS AND DESIGNERS

Kambli, Johann Melchior
1718–83 German furniture maker and designer of interior decorations and bronze mounts. The main founder of German Rococo. From 1746 worked for Frederick the Great. Furniture remarkable for the quality and fantasy of its mounts. Also made furniture to Nahl's designs and produced mounts.

Kent, William
c1684–1748 English architect, landscape designer, interior decorator and furniture designer. Architecture strongly influenced by Inigo Jones but furniture Italianate in its massive form and Baroque motifs. Carving, gilding and marble combined created the opulence of his major pieces.

Klint, Kaare
1888–1954 Danish furniture designer. Pioneered modern rational Scandinavian furniture design.

Le Corbusier, Charles Edouard Jeanneret
1887–1965 Born Switzerland, worked much in France. Architect and furniture designer. From 1926 designed furniture in collaboration with his brother, Pierre Jeanneret, and with Charlotte Perriand. In "Pavillon de l'Esprit Nouveau" in the 1925 Paris Exhibition he displayed modern furniture and Thonet's bentwood chairs together; the first sign in France of the Modernist approach to room design.

Mackintosh, Charles Rennie
1868–1928 Scottish architect and designer. Furniture, non-functional in approach, influenced by Japanese style of E. W. Godwin particularly in use of long thin members, and often decorated with Art-Nouveau motifs of tendrils and flowers. Craftsmanship not excellent. Work more influential in Germany and Austria than in England.

Maggiolini, Giuseppe
1738–1814 Italian furniture maker. Best-known for fine marquetry and quality of craftsmanship. Worked for rulers of Milan, whether Austrian or French, in a restrained Neoclassical style. A few signed pieces survive.

Majorelle, Louis
1859–1926 French furniture designer. Inherited a furniture workshop; became the leading producer of Art Nouveau furniture in France c1900. Furniture opulent, well-designed, well-executed. Post World War I he adopted a more severe, geometric style, but still produced luxury furnishings.

Marot, Daniel
1663–1752 Born France. Architect and designer. Worked mainly in Holland; 1694 to 1698 worked in England for William III. Introduced grand Baroque style to England and Holland. Beds particularly are complex confections of carving and drapery. Possibly responsible for the proportions – high back and short legs – of William and Mary chairs.

Martin, Guillaume
d1749
Etienne-Simon
d1770
Julien
d1783
Robert
1706–66. French furniture designers and makers. Invented *vernis Martin*, a delicate European lacquer with which whole pieces of furniture were painted. It included a wide range of colors and sometimes a fine spray of gold dust in the final layers.

Mies van der Rohe, Ludwig
1886–1969 German architect and furniture designer. Worked in the US from 1938. Most famous furniture designs (all extremely elegant), are for a cantilever tubular steel chair in 1926 and the Barcelona chair of 1929, perhaps the finest design of the first half of the 20th century.

Oeben, Jean François

c1721–63. Born in Germany, Oeben moved to Paris and became the most important cabinet-maker of his day. Work combines superb *trompe l'oeil* marquetry, much later exchanged for geometrical marquetry, with mechanical ingenuity. Most famous piece probably the Bureau du Roi Louis XV at Versailles; this was completed after his death by his assistant Riesener.

Percier, Charles

1764–1838 and

Fontaine, Pierre-François Leonard

1762–1853 French designers. They share responsibility for creating the French Empire style and for arranging the elaborate living stage sets for Napoleon. Draperies and antique motifs employed lavishly in their work. Their *"Recueil des décorations intérieurs"* of 1801 is the first and fullest representation of the style.

Phyfe, Duncan

1768–1854 Born Scotland. Became America's best known furniture maker and designer. Workshops in New York very large, run on factory system. Nevertheless, quality of his pieces high until 1830s when mahogany was replaced by cheaper woods. Work follows English and European fashions; meritorious rather than exciting or original.

Piffetti, Pietro

c1700–77 Italian furniture maker and designer. Best known work executed 1731 on for the Royal Court at Turin. At first strongly influenced by Juvara's Baroque designs but after mid-1730s developed his own version of Rococo. Work much more fussy than French or German Rococo and pieces encrusted with over-plentiful etched ivory, gilt and mother-of-pearl. Very high-quality craftsmanship.

Pugin, Augustus Welby Northmore

1812–52 English architect and designer. In the vanguard of the Gothic revival, had a much more precise understanding of Gothic work than any of his predecessors. Insisted on solid craftsmanship and on attention to authentic Gothic detail. His *Gothic Furniture in the style of the 15th century* (1835) and *The true Principle of Pointed or Christian Architecture* of 1841 are landmarks in the development of 19th-century taste.

Riesener, Jean-Henri

1734–1806 Born in Germany. Furniture maker and designer. Entered Oeben's workshop in Paris c1754, took it over on Oeben's death. Became *Ébéniste du Roi* 1774. Probably the finest of all Louis XVI cabinet-makers. Early works are in Oeben's style; he completed a number of Oeben's pieces after his death, including the Bureau du Roi Louis XV and the similar desk for King Stanislas Lesczynski. Designed and made furniture entirely in his own workshop, using his own bronze casters for the mounts. Quality of his design and workmanship unsurpassed. Name associated with very best furniture in Louis XVI style.

Rietveld, Gerrit Thomas

1888–1964 Dutch architect and furniture designer. From 1917 he created an abstract sculptural style for furniture; associated with the de Stijl group of artists. Reacted against functionalism and the truth-to-materials ideas promulgated by the Arts and Crafts Movement. Furniture is antifunctional, wood painted in brilliant primary colors. Each piece a work of art, not a useful object.

Risenburgh, Bernard II van

c1700–65/7 French cabinet-maker and designer who signed his work "B.V.R.B". Work, mainly in the Rococo style, carries elegant combinations of Sèvres ware, oriental lacquer, vernis Martin and fine wooden marquetries. Worked for *marchand-merciers* but his excellent work found its way to French and foreign courts.

MAKERS AND DESIGNERS

Roentgen, Abraham
1711–93 and
Roentgen, David
1743–1807 German furniture makers
and designers. Abraham, David's father,
worked in England and Paris for short
periods before founding the family firm
at Neuwied in 1750. Abraham was just
a good designer and maker of furniture;
David, who took over the management
of the business in 1768, was both a fine
designer and brilliant businessman. His
furniture is marked by fine marquetry,
good bronzes and, in the grandest
pieces by astonishing opulence and
monumentality. Depots were
established in Vienna, Paris, Berlin,
Kassel, Gotha and Altenburg: he
became the best-known cabinet-maker
of his time. He traveled exclusively to
further his business: best customers
included Catherine II of Russia, Louis
XVI, Marie Antoinette.

Ruhlmann, Jacques-Émile
1879–1933 French interior decorator
and furniture designer. Produced most
luxurious of European furniture in 1920s
and early 1930s. Methods of
production, where very highest standard
of craftsmanship was applied to the
most expensive materials (Caucasian
burr walnut, macassar ebony, ivory,
shagreen) recall the 18th century.
Designs are often based on an 18th-
century or, later, Empire sense of
proportion, with Art Deco motifs.

Saarinen, Eero
1910–61 b Finland. American architect
and furniture designer. Created furniture
in organic forms pressed out of plastic
or, where necessary, cast in metal.
Furniture distinguished by its grace,
best exemplified by the fiber-glass and
metal "tulip" chairs and tables with
delicate, wine-glass-like stems.

Sambin, Hugues
c1520–c1601 French architect, woodcarver and designer. Worked in Dijon
where carried out architectural
commissions. In 1572 published a series
of designs for terms (columns in the
form of standing human half figures,
where lower halves merge into
pedestals). Made no furniture himself
but Mannerist decoration influenced
ornament of French furniture for half a
century.

Savery, William
1721–88 American furniture maker. One
of the major furniture makers of
Philadelphia. Work at its most elaborate
strongly influenced by Chippendale.
Particularly well known for his chairs.

Schinkel, Karl Friedrich
1781–1841 German architect and
furniture designer. Furniture much
underrated in comparison with his
architecture. Neo-Greek, neo-Roman
and neo-Gothic styles remarkably
functional and attractive. Used sound
constructions and simple forms
(whatever their derivation) to produce
furniture with all the best qualities of
following Biedermeier period together
with an elegance which is his own.

Sheraton, Thomas
1751–1806 English furniture designer.
No furniture is known by him: he
formulated later English Neoclassicism,
borrowing from Adam and Hepplewhite
creating rather feminine forms. *The
Cabinet-maker and Upholsterer's
Drawing Book* (1791, reprinted 1794
and 1802) reproduces a range of pieces,
very simple to very complex, all of great
delicacy. Most ornate pieces use paint
and marquetry. Simpler pieces rely on
good lines and exquisite wood. Later
pieces are of increasing eccentricity as
he became mad: but in *"Cabinet
Dictionary"* (1803) and the published
parts of *Cabinet-Maker, Upholsterer and
General Artists' Encyclopaedia*
(1804–06) he showed the fullest
formulation of English Regency style.

Thonet, Michael
1796–1871 German furniture designer
and industrialist. Thonet began work as

a parquetry designer, became a Biedermeier cabinet-maker, ended up as owner of the world's largest manufactory of cheap furniture. In 1841 he patented the steam bending of beechwood strips for furniture; in 1859 in Vienna he produced the chair known as Thonet no. 14, a chair made purely of bentwood sections and caned seat, which could be assembled easily anywhere. It is the largest selling chair ever made.

Vile, William
1700–67 and
Cobb, John
c1710–78 English furniture makers and interior decorators who went into partnership c1750. In 1761 Vile became cabinet-maker to the Royal household. Much of their best furniture made for the crown. Their carved mahogany and marquetries of ivory and precious woods are of the very highest quality. Work mainly in a restrained Rococo but moved to delicate Neoclassicism in later works by Cobb.

Voysey, Charles Francis Annesley
1857–1941 English architect and designer. Furniture stands part-way between ideas of William Morris and shapes of Art Nouveau. Wood displays natural properties but Japonaiserie, derived from E. W. Godwin, sometimes evident in thin, square-section free-standing, pillars of sideboards. Simple country quality combines with highly developed sense of proportion.

Vredeman de Vries, Hans
1527–c1604 Flemish architectural ornamentalist, painter and designer. Published 1565 the largest collection of furniture designs of the 16th century. Designs reflect contemporary popular patterns. Some were extremely simple, all look very heavy, and ornament when present is overelaborate and Mannerist. Paul his son produced similar designs in 1630.

Wegner, Hans
b1914 Danish architect, furniture maker and designer. A craftsman too, his furniture is beautifully constructed. Uses wood in preference to synthetic materials; often includes handmade elements. The master craftsman with whom he has been most associated is Johannes Hansen.

Weisweiler, Adam
c1750–c1810 German-born cabinet-maker and furniture designer. Worked in France, master *ébéniste* in 1778. Worked mainly for Daguerre, influential *marchand-mercier*, through whom his work found its way to the French Court and the English Prince Regent. Work is exquisite. Was particularly fond of black and gold Japanese lacquer panels and Sèvres placques as decorative elements in his furniture and made considerable use of gilding. Possibly Gouthière designed some of his mounts. Re-used *pietre dure* plaques from reign of Louis XIV in some pieces. Most pieces small-scale with the detail and delicacy of jewelry.

Wright, Frank Lloyd
1867–1959 American architect and designer. Early furniture from turn of the century shares Arts and Crafts' concern for "fidelity to materials", particularly wood. Both his wood and metal furniture of this time is functional, though unconcerned with main factory production, furniture for each of his buildings being designed as a "one-off" job. Later furniture became bizarre; sculpture, not furniture.

GLOSSARY

Acanthus leaves Stylized leaf ornaments derived from the capitals of Corinthian columns and found on Neoclassical furniture.

Antwerp cabinet Cabinet-on-stand made mainly in 17th-century Netherlands but copied in England, France, Spain and Italy.

Arabesque marquetry Mainly Spanish and Portuguese decoration of 16th and 17th centuries spreading to Northern Europe in late 17th and early 18th centuries, consisting of intertwining lines. Derived from Moorish work.

Armoire Wardrobe or enclosed cupboard.

Athénienne French Neoclassical or Empire three-legged free-standing wash-stand.

Aumbry Late Medieval food cupboard.

Auricular style A 17th-century Netherlandish style of decoration, in which boneless, cartilaginous forms were used.

Ball foot Foot in the shape of a ball. Often used in the 17th century.

Beeldenkast Early 17th century Netherlandish cabinet decorated with carved scenes and human figures.

Bergère French 18th- and 19th-century armchair with enclosed arms.

Block-front An 18th-century New England form of decorating the front of cabinets, lowboys, highboys, made up of two convex rectangular, or apse-ended rectangular sections flanking one concave but similar section.

Bombé Displaying round curves. Used particularly of some 18th-century case furniture.

Bonheurs du jour French or English 18th-century ladies' desks with the drawers in a raised section at the back. A small secretaire.

Buhl work A 19th-century style of decorating furniture derived from that of Andre-Charles Boulle.

Bun foot Foot shaped like a flattened globe.

Burr woods Finely figured woods cut from burrs or excrescences.

Cabochon ornament A raised oval sculptural furniture decoration.

Cabriole leg Curved leg brought to Europe from China in the late 17th century and used in Europe until the introduction of Neoclassicism.

Canapée An 18th-century French sofa.

Caquetoire A 16th-century trapezoidal seated chair.

Carcase The structural body of a piece of veneered furniture.

Caryatid Sculpted female supporting figure.

Casapanca A 16th-century Italian combination chest and seat with a low back and arms.

Cassone Italian 15th- 16th- or 17th-century marriage chests, usually made in pairs.

Champlevé Technique of enameling in which the cells containing the enamel are cut into the metal.

Chasing Embossing or engraving metal in relief.

Chinoiserie European work in a Chinese or psuedo-Chinese style.

Chip carving Carved ornament in wood, often geometric in shape, made by chipping out sections of wood.

Claw and ball foot Foot shaped like a claw clutching a ball. Much used in England in the first two-thirds of the 18th century.

Cloisonné Technique of enameling in which the cells containing the enamel are formed by attaching wire to the surface of the metal.

Commode Chest-of-drawers.

Coromandel lacquer The 17th- and 18th-century name for the colored incised lacquers of China imported to Europe via the Coromandel coast of India.

Credenza Italian sideboard.

Damascening Method of decorating metal by beating gold or silver wire into an engraved or cut pattern.

Duchesse A short daybed arranged like a *bergère* chair with a lengthened seat.

Ébéniste French cabinet-maker.

Egg and dart Ornament of carved alternate egg and dart shapes used on Neoclassical furniture, derived from an original Greek motif.

Embossing Method of decorating metal by beating a pattern in relief from the back.

Enameling Method of decorating metal by fusing a glassy substance onto it.

Encoignure French standing corner cupboard. They were often made in pairs with a matching commode.

Endive marquetry Marquetry made into ragged leaf-forms.

Faience Glazed and decorated earthenware, originally Italian.

Fall-front (drop-front) The panel of a desk which falls to make a writing surface.

Farthingale chair Late 16th-century chair made without arms, supposedly to accommodate the wide skirts of the period.

Fasces The bundle of rods from the center of which an axe head protrudes, carried before a Roman lictor, adopted as a decorative motif in Neoclassical work.

Feather banding (herringbone banding) Border veneer in which the grain is set diagonally like the filaments of a feather or a series of fish bones.

Gadrooning Carved border ornament of straight or angled loofah shapes.

Gesso Size applied to furniture before gilt is applied.

Grotesques Decorations of the sort discovered in the early 16th century in the excavations of Nero's Golden House. So called because the rooms were underground: grottoes. Popular in the Neoclassical period.

Guadamecil leather Spanish 16th-century tooled and colored leather used as chair covering.

Guéridon French candlestand, sometimes doubling as a worktable.

Highboy American 18th-century tall chest-of-drawers.

Husk Classical ornament resembling a wheat or hazelnut husk, usually arranged in strings. Employed on Neoclassical furniture.

Incised carving Carving where the pattern is cut as a thin line into the wood.

Inlay Decoration of pieces of wood set into a design excavated in the supporting wood.

Intarsia Complex pictorial inlay or marquetry.

Japanning European imitation of oriental lacquer.

Kas An 18th-century Pennsylvanian Dutch painted cupboard.

K'ang Raised brick platform at one end of a Chinese room, heated from below in winter, used as a bed and a seat.

Klismos chair Greek chair with saber legs back and front and curved horizontal back support. The model for Regency and Directory chairs.

Kneehole desk Desk with drawers or cupboards flanking the user's lower limbs.

Lac burgauté Lacquer where small pieces of mother-of-pearl are pressed into the lacquer when wet and the surface flattened by polishing.

Lacquer Varnish made of the resin of *Rhus vernicifera* in China and Japan and applied in layers to give a brilliant surface to, usually wooden, furniture.

Ladderback chair Chair, the back of which consists of horizontal slats formed to resemble a ladder.

Laminated wood Wood formed of glued or bonded veneers arranged with their grains running in parallel.

Linenfold paneling Wall-paneling decorated with a raised design resembling folded linen.

Lowboy American low chest-of-drawers.

Marlborough leg Straight leg with projecting (all round) square foot. Used in 18th century England and America.

Marquetry Veneer of a complex, usually pictorial, pattern, often using a number of different woods or other organic or mineral materials.

Marquise An 18th-century French sofa, seating two persons.

Méridienne Directory daybed with either one or two curled-over arm ends.

Menuisier French chair-maker.

Molding Sculpted band-shaped relief decoration.

GLOSSARY

Mortise The projection which fits into the hole or tenon to form a mortise and tenon joint.

Mudejar Late 15th-century style of decoration used in Spain and Portugal, showing strong Moorish influence.

Niello Technique of decorating metal with a black inlay by fusing an alloy of various metals into an engraved design.

Ormolu Gilded bronze, often used for mounts.

Ottomane Louis XV (and later) oval seated sofa with back and arms forming a continuous curve.

Oyster shell veneer Wooden veneer usually cut from small branches of trees like laburnum, so that each separate veneer resembles an oyster shell. Often grouped in patterns on late 17th-century Dutch and English cabinets.

Pad foot Club foot set on a disk.

Paintbrush foot An 18th-century American foot resembling a paint-brush head pressed gently against a hard surface.

Palmette Classical decoration resembling a fan or a formalized palm-leaf. Used on Neoclassical furniture.

Papeleira A vargueño without the fall front.

Papier mâché A mixture of pounded glue and paper molded and dried; often used inaccurately to describe furniture made of glued paper laminations. Very popular in the 19th century.

Parquetry Simple geometrical marquetry, of one or several kinds of wood.

Patera Classical rounded or oval decoration used on Neoclassical furniture.

Pembroke table Table with folding side flaps on brackets which fold back against a central drawer. The table may be oval or rectangular when flaps are raised.

Pierced carving Carving which penetrates right through the wood.

Pietre dure Decorative panels of semi-precious stones and marbles.

Plateresque Spanish early Renaissance patterns.

Relief carving Carving in which the design stands proud of the surface.

Repoussé work Raised decoration on metal produced by beating from the back and finished by chasing or engraving on the front.

Romayne work Renaissance decoration of profile heads in medallions.

Saber leg Leg with a backward or forward sweep from top to bottom.

Scagliola Substitute marble made from marble paste.

Secretary Desk with drawers above and to the rear of the writing surface.

Shagreen Dyed shark skin.

Shield back Chair-back in the shape of a shield used in England in the late 18th century.

Sillón de cadera Commonest sort of chair in Spain and Portugal in the 16th and 17th centuries, in shape X frame, usually folding.

Sillón de fraileros Rectangular or square Spanish or Portuguese chair, contemporary with *sillón de cadera*. Adapted from ecclesiastical model.

Singeries Decorative patterns including figures of monkeys acting or dressed like human beings. Probably invented by Bérain.

Splat Vertical member in the back of a chair. Sometimes pierced.

Strapwork Low relief carving of flat interweaving ribbons, which originated in the 16th-century Low Countries or in Germany. Much used throughout 16th and early 17th centuries there and in England.

Stretcher Member fitted low down to chair or table legs to brace them.

String-banding Very fine strip of veneer set as a border between other wider sections of veneer.

Tables dormants Large fixed dining tables in use in Europe by the 14th century.

Tambour front Roll-top front for a desk, made of canvas with slats of wood glued over it.

Tenon Hole into which the mortise fits in a mortise and tenon joint.

Tester Wooden or fabric canopy for a bed, supported on poles or suspended from the ceiling.

Turkey work Knotted fabric, often with geometrical or pictorial designs, made in Europe in the 16th and 17th centuries in imitation of Turkish carpet knotting. Used for chair upholstery, cushions, bedcovers.

Turning Craft of producing plain or decorated circular section wooden members with the use of the lathe.

Vargueño Spanish 16th- or 17th-century writing desk with a fall-front flap, placed on a stand.

Veneer Thin slice of decorative wood applied to a carcase of wood structurally more sound but less attractive.

Verre eglomisé Painted glass backed by metal foil, usually gold or silver so that both paint and metal show through the glass.

Vernis Martin An 18th-century European lacquer substitute invented and used by the Martin brothers in Paris.

Volute Classical ornament of a spiral scroll usually seen in profile. Used on Renaissance and Neoclassical furniture.

Voyeuse An 18th-century chair with padded top rail to the back. Supposedly to be lent on by an observer while the occupant of the chair was playing cards.

Wave mouldings Deeply incised bands of carving showing a straight or curved series of lines advancing like a series of waves. Used as a border along top edge of some Neoclassical furniture.

ACKNOWLEDGMENTS

Unless otherwise stated all the illustrations on a given page are credited to the same source.

The photograph on page 24 is reproduced by gracious permission of H.M. Queen Elizabeth II Copyright reserved. Other photographs are reproduced by permission of American Museum in Britain, Bath page 178–179, 182, 211; Ashmolean Museum, Oxford page 26, 49, 59, 66, 126, 223; Bavaria Verlag, Munich page 109; Bowes Museum, Co Durham page 212; Trustees of the British Museum, London page 53, 63; Casa Rezzonica, Venice page 84; Trustees of the Chatsworth Settlement page 153; Christie's, London page 106; Cooper-Bridgeman Library, London page 17, 31, 32, 60, 71, 88, 162, 203, 207, 208, 215, 217, 229; Courtauld Institute Galleries, London page 76; Design Council, London page 29, 228, 234, 230–231, 233, 240, 241, 242; Dulwich College, London page 93; Robert Harding Associates, London page 44, 45; Controller of H.M. Stationery Office, London Crown Copyright page 69, 213; Michael Holford, London page 46, 48, 51, 55, 64–65; A. F. Kersting, London page 73; Kettle's Yard, Cambridge page 96; Landesmuseum, Munster page 108; Mansell Collection, London page 36; Musée du Louvre, Paris page 38t, 195; Musées Royaux d'Art et d'Histoire, Brussels/A.C.L. page 50; Museum of Modern Art, New York Gift of the manufacturer, Thonet Industries Inc page 222; National Trust, London page 118, 145, 146, 147, 148, 154–155, 157, 199r, 200–201; National Trust Waddesdon Manor, Aylesbury page 23, 132–133, 138; Orbis Picture Library, London page 10, 224; Osterreichische Nationalbibliothek, Vienna page 68; Peruvian Embassy, London/Paul Forrester page 191; Picturepoint Ltd, London page 173; Ann Ronan Picture Library, page 15, 16; Rijksmuseum, Amsterdam page 101; Royal Pavillion Art Gallery and Museums, Brighton page 32–33; Scala, Florence page 83, 85, 87, 129; Schonbrunn Palace, Vienna page 112; Staatlichen Schlosser und Garten, Berlin page 111; Victoria and Albert Museum, London page 22, 27, 30, 37, 62, 72, 78, 80, 81, 92, 94, 104, 105, 110, 119, 123, 143, 144, 149, 158, 164, 165, 172, 189, 199l, 210, 214, 216, 219r, 236, 237; Victoria and Albert Museum, London/Paul Forrester page 115, 139, 152, 156, 161; Trustees of the Wallace Collection, London page 25, 38b, 125, 130, 137; Weidenfeld and Nicholson, London page 89; Weidenfeld and Nicholson/The Duke of Northumberland page 121; Weidenfeld and Nicholson/Mr and Mrs Brian Housden page 225; Jeremy Whitaker page 100.

Illustrations by: Roger Gorringe, page 12, 40, 41, 42, 43, 95, 98, 103, 169, 171, 180, 181, 182, 185, 187, 218, 239: Malcolm McGregor, page 18, 79, 174, 175, 176; Oxford Illustrators page 18, 19, 57, 74, 90, 116, 141, 160, 195, 205, 220, 227.

The publishers have attempted to observe the legal requirements with respect to the rights of the suppliers of photographic materials. Nevertheless persons who have claims are invited to apply to the publishers.

INDEX